Michael's
THE   NEW GUIDE
BARCELONA

GW00692085

THE NEW GUIDE
Michael's
BARCELONA

Managing Editor
Michael Shichor

Series Editor
Amir Shichor

INBAL TRAVEL INFORMATION LTD.

Inbal Travel Information Ltd.
P.O.Box 1870 Ramat Gan 52117
Israel

Intl. ISBN 965-288-112-0

Text: Shlomo Papirblat
        Menachem (Chemi) Shkolnik
Graphic design: Michel Opatowski
Cover design: Bill Stone
Photography: Yossi Shrem
Photo editor: Claudio Nutkiewicz
Editorial: Sharona Johan, Or Rinat, Lisa Stone
D.T.P.: Irit Bahalul
Maps: Orit Avni, Rina Waserman
Printed by Havatzelet Press Ltd.

Distributed in the United Kingdom by:
Kuperard (London) Ltd.
9 Hampstead West
224 Iverson Road
West Hampstead
London NW6 2HL

U.K. ISBN 1-85733-094-3

CONTENTS

TABLE OF MAPS

Since the return of Spain to a democratic system of government, following General Franco's death in 1975, it has started to adjust to the great many changes in the modern European community and to become an important and ever more active member of this community. Against the background of these fast developments Barcelona emerges, undoubtedly, as having an important and central role.

The visitor to Barcelona will find there one of the most important ports in Europe. This old and historic port from where Columbus launched his historic voyage has recently become, once again, a bustling commercial and industrial center.

But this lively city is not only a center of industry and commerce. It is also and has been, for many years, a cultural center and home (at least temporarily) for many great artists. Author Gabriel Garcia Marquez, painters Pablo Picasso and Joan Miro, cellist Pablo Casals – they all lived and worked here, their work effected by the city and its atmosphere. Most distinguished is, of course, Antoni Gaudí, the master architect, who left his mark on many of Barcelona's buildings, adding a unique modernist touch to a city already full of beautiful older structures.

Our staff of researchers and writers, headed by the journalist Shlomo Papirblat and the traveler Chemi Shkolnik, made every possible effort to compile a comprehensive Guide, in order to introduce you to the many sights and perfumes of this charming city. Our aim is to give you a deeper understanding of Barcelona, to lead you to its best and most fascinating attractions and to ensure that you derive maximum pleasure from your trip. We are sure that the effort invested in compiling this Guide will be justified by your enhanced enjoyment.

Michael Shichor

Using this Guide

In order to reap maximum benefit from the information in this Guide, we advise the traveler to carefully read the following advice. The facts contained in this book were compiled to help the tourist find his or her way around and to ensure that he enjoys his stay to the upmost.

The Introduction will supply you with details which will help you to make the early decisions and arrangements for your trip. We advise you to carefully review the material, so that you will be more organized and set for your visit. Upon arrival in Barcelona, you will already feel familiar and comfortable with the city, more so than otherwise would have been the case.

The basic guideline in all "MICHAEL'S GUIDE" publications is to survey places in a primarily geographical sequence. The detailed introductory chapters discuss general topics and specific aspects of getting organized. The tour routes, laid out geographically, lead the visitor up and down the city's streets, providing a survey of the sites and calling attention to all those details which deepen one's familiarity with Barcelona, and make a visit there so much more enjoyable. At the end of each chapter is a section called "Additional points of interest", which relates to sites located in the vicinity of that tour route.

Since Barcelona is highly esteemed for its gourmet cuisine, Spanish wines, fine shopping and entertainment, we have devoted a special chapter to "Making the most of your stay" in the city. Here you will find a broad range of possibilities, to suit your budget, which will help you enjoy your stay.

A concise list of "musts" follows, describing those sites without which a visit to Barcelona is not complete.

The reader will notice that certain facts tend to recur. This is deliberate; it enables the tourist who starts out from a point other than the one we choose, to be no less informed. The result is a flexibility in personal planning.

The rich collection of maps covers the tour routes and special attractions in great detail. Especially prepared for this book, they will certainly add to the efficiency and pleasure of your exploration of Barcelona.

A short chapter is provided on shopping, entertainment, restaurants, and the other essences of this city. These will help visitors fill their suitcases and stomachs – and empty their wallets – comprehensively, thoroughly, and as economically as possible. Here again, a broad spectrum of possibilities is provided, taking the budgets of all travelers into consideration (while guaranteeing a most enjoyable visit).

To further facilitate the use of this Guide, we have included a detailed index. It includes all the major sites mentioned throughout the book. Consult the index to find something by name and it will refer you to the place where it is mentioned in greatest detail.

During your visit you will see and experience many things – we have therefore left several blank pages at the back of the Guide. These are for you, to jot down those special experiences of people and places, feelings and significant happenings along the way.

Because times and cities are dynamic, an important rule of thumb when traveling, and especially when visiting a vibrant city like Barcelona, should be to consult local sources of information. Tourists are liable to encounter certain inaccuracies in this Guide and for these, we apologize.

The producer of a guide of this type assumes a great responsibility: that of presenting the right information in a way which allows for an easy, safe and economical visit. For this purpose, we have included a short questionnaire and will be most grateful for those who will take the time to complete it and send it to us.

Have a pleasant and exciting trip – Bon Voyage!

PART ONE –
GETTING TO KNOW BARCELONA

History

The Iberian tribes were the first in recorded history to have settled in what is now called Barcelona. Apparently, they came from the Sahara region and arrived in the Iberian Peninsula (which bears their name) during the Neolithic period. Here, they intermingled with the Celtic tribes which had come from the north. A group of these nomadic tribes settled on the slopes of Mt. Montjuïc, in the southwestern part of the present city.

Seafarers of the ancient world who crossed the Mediterranean, first Phoenicians and then Greeks, arrived at a later date. In their search for new trade routes, they landed on these shores and it was here that they set up trading posts. Among the things they introduced were the olive tree and the grape vine, the coining of money and the Greek alphabet. Signs of these physical and cultural innovations are evident to this day.

At the end of the third century BC, during the Second Punic War, Scipio Africanus "the elder", army commander and later Roman consul, captured the area on his way to subdue Carthage (which posed a threat under the leadership of Hannibal). At that time, Barcelona was called Barcino, after the military leader Hamilcar Barca, father of Hannibal.

As was their custom, the Romans brought their developed urban culture with them and established a city alongside the Iberian settlement. But the Iberian tribes did not accept them passively and responded with prolonged guerrilla warfare. During the first century BC the Roman garrison was forced to mount fierce battles against them on several occasions. In the year 27 BC, Augustus came to the Iberian Peninsula in order to restore order. One of the reasons that he wanted to deal with the Spanish problem in person was the discovery of gold mines in the area.

Around the year 14 BC the situation stabilized, but only after a second campaign in Spain undertaken by Augustus at the

head of a large army. During the course of this campaign, Augustus also succeeded in subduing the rebel leader Corcotta. The Romans offered a large prize to whoever would bring them his head and, one day, to their surprise, Corcotta arrived at Augustus' tent and said: "Here is my head; give me the prize." The Roman leader chose to pardon him, which proved to be a wise political decision. Spain became a docile Roman province, which absorbed many ex-Roman legionnaires as settlers. Augustus is commemorated in a temple named after him, the remains of which still exist in the city.

Later, the disintegration and surrender of the Roman Empire to the tribes, who came from the north inevitably left its mark on the history of Barcelona as well. The Visigoths, who came south from the region of the Danube, arrived at Rome in the year 410AD, and reached Spain five years later. For a short time, the new conquerors made Barcelona their regional capital; this was the first recognition of its importance. After the Visigoth King, Reccared I, converted to Christianity at the end of the sixth century, the Christian church held a convention in the city. Christians had first appeared here as early as the first century.

In the year 713, along with most of the Iberian Peninsula, Barcelona fell to the Moslems (the Moors who came from North Africa). The new conquerors called the city Bargelona, according to the Arabic. Along with the name, the Arabs also brought their culture and architecture. The way of life changed, but the Christian inhabitants were not ready to accept these changes without a struggle. Beginning in 781 revolts and uprisings occurred in Barcelona, influenced in great part by the city's Frankish neighbors to the north. Finally the city was conquered by the Frankish King Charlemagne (Charles I) in the year 801. It became the district capital of the region then called the "Spanish March", which occupied more or less the area that constitutes the district of Catalonia today.

When the power of the Frankish kingdom in the area weakened, near the end of the ninth century, Barcelona became an independent earldom. It continued to be threatened by the Moslems and was actually conquered by them twice, for short periods, at the beginning of the tenth century.

The Middle Ages find Barcelona flourishing, both economically and culturally. The Catalonian ruler, Ramón Berenguer I, signed the legislation known as the "Ustages" in 1068 in Barcelona, thus conferring on the city a place of honor in the annals of law. At this time, the Catalonian rulers adopted the knightly emblem of four vertical red stripes on a red background, which later became the Catalonian flag called *Senyera*.

Ramón Berenguer III, who ruled from 1096-1131, increased the influence of the dukedom and concluded treaties with the independent state of Provence and with Italian rulers. Ramón Berenguer IV (1131-1162) was very active and became the king of Aragón, after his successful political marriage to the princess of the House of Aragón. The dukedom was known then as "Greater Catalonia" and included both Catalonia and Aragón, although Aragón retained independent institutions and its own language.

The port of Barcelona became the main gateway for sea trade from Christian Spain, and the city's ships connected it with all the cities of the Mediterranean Basin, as far as Egypt and Constantinople. Political and economic "ambassadors" of Barcelona sat in the main port cities of the various states and contributed to the growth of commerce. At that time,

Barcelona successfully competed even with Venice and Genoa. "The Book of Nautical Law", which served as one of the foundations of international maritime law, was compiled by the ship captains of Barcelona during this period. There was further evidence of the preeminence of Barcelona seafaring when later, at the beginning of the sixteenth century, the first body in history to deal with marine insurance was established here.

In the thirteenth century, Barcelona, as part of "Greater Catalonia", exploited its economic power to embark on a path of military conquest. Led by King Jeime I, the conqueror, it annexed the Balearic Islands, the kingdom of Valencia, Sicily, and Sardinia. The Catalonian dynasty even ruled over the Athenian dukedom between 1311-1386.

But, along with its prosperity, Barcelona also knew difficult and cruel times. In 1348, a terrible plague broke out in Catalonia, which caused the death of about one third of the inhabitants. Those who remained alive had only a brief respite before the Spanish civil wars broke out. In 1359, Barcelona residents witnessed a sea battle off its shores which lasted for three full days. The battle entered the history books as the "Port Battle" between the fleets of Pedro I, King of Aragón and Catalonia, and Pedro IV, King of Castile.

King Martin I, the last of the dynasty of the House of Barcelona and Aragón, died in 1410, leaving no heirs. For the next two years, the struggles for succession continued among noblemen of the kingdom, until the crown was placed on the head of the Castilian prince, Ferdinand I. This was totally at odds with the wishes of the Catalonians and left numerous scars in its wake.

The rebellious character of Barcelona, which is an integral part of its history, manifested itself again between 1460-1470, to the city's detriment. The people of Barcelona revolted against King Juan II, and the long, cruel struggle ended only when the city was afforded certain rights and tax privileges. But the ensuing debilitation of the city was the start of its decline.

The end of the fifteenth century brought two additional factors in the deterioration of Barcelona's situation. Against the background of the marriage of Ferdinand II and Isabella, and the unification of the Castilian and Aragónian kingdoms, new sea routes were discovered – to America and to India (around the Horn of Africa), causing the center of commerce with the Spanish colonies to shift to the ports of Seville and Cadiz. The Mediterranean Sea lost its economic lure to the Atlantic Ocean. And, the second unfortunate factor was the establishment in Barcelona of a center of the Inquisition, which persecuted and banished Marrano Jews, thereby damaging the economic structure in which they had been very active.

Against this background, unrest increased in Barcelona

and throughout Catalonia, and there was a growing inclination for separation from the Castilian government. Toward the middle of the seventeenth century, a revolt of citizens against King Philip IV broke out. Representatives of the rebels turned to the king of France, asking him to become the protector of the district. But Philip IV did not yield. Bloody battles ensued in the area, lasting more than ten years. Eventually, after a cruel blockade of the city, Barcelona surrendered. Although the agreements signed after the battles had subsided left Catalonia with some of its

The glorious nautical history is commemorated at the Maritime Museum

Barcelona's Triumph Arch

autonomous laws intact, it then lost, once and for all, two of its districts in the northern Pyrenees, Rossello and Cerdanya. An echo of this unrest is found in the national anthem of Catalonia, "The Reapers" *Els Segadors*.

Bearing these scars, Barcelona found itself swept up in the War of Spanish Succession. This occurred after the death of Charles II, who left no heirs. In 1700 the son of the French heir Philip d'Anjou, ascended the throne of Spain as King Philip V. He, of course, brought with him a French retinue and dispatched French forces to the Spanish lowlands. He assigned France important commercial privileges in all the crown colonies of Spain. This unified French and Spanish force provoked the "Grand Alliance" of England, Austria, and Holland into action. They wanted the Spanish throne for the Archduke Charles of the House of Hapsburg. A full-scale war broke out. Barcelona, of course, supported the archduke, who landed on its shores in 1705 at the head of an Austrian force. The battles took place throughout Spain, with first one side, and then the other, gaining the upper hand. But in 1711 the Archduke, offered the throne of the German Kaiser, became Charles VI. Three years later, on September 11, 1714, following the withdrawal of the Austrian forces from Barcelona, the city fell to Philip V, despite the valiant stand of its citizens. The courage of the defenders and their hopeless struggle turned this day into the national holiday of Catalonia, which is still celebrated every year.

Revenge was swift. The local legislative body was dispersed, the Catalonian language lost its official status, and the University of Barcelona was closed. At the same time, there was an economic resurgence (the textile branch and brandy manufacture flourished), which reached its height toward the end of the eighteenth century. Economic prosperity was further generated when, in 1778, enlightened King Charles III cancelled the Sevillian monopoly in everything related to commerce with the colonies. The renewed prosperity is clearly shown in population records of the city: in 1717 it had 35,000 inhabitants, while in 1787, there were already about 111,000.

However, peace and prosperity did not last long. The bloodletting of the Spanish civil wars in the nineteenth century caused Barcelona much damage, especially in 1842 when, after it had consistently supported the liberal forces, it found itself confronting the dictatorial general Esparetro. Events unfolded as follows: King Ferdinand VII was crowned in 1814, after the downfall of Napoleon. In 1829, a daughter Isabella was born to him (who eventually proved to have been born under a baleful star). Ferdinand died when she was only four years old, and her mother, Maria Christina, became Regent, with the support of the liberal trends in Spain. But the brother of the deceased king, Don Carlos invoked a Spanish law from 1713, according to which a female

may not inherit the throne, and proceeded to crown himself King Charles V. Inevitably, civil war broke out. Because of the division among the Carlists, it ended in the victory of Maria Christina. But the trauma had weakened her, and it was now that General Espartero, a war hero, seized power. Barcelona rebelled against his tyrannical rule as royal regent and suffered greatly at his hand in return.

It was in the economic sphere that the city regained its vitality, but, at the same time, negative processes were initiated which augured future difficulties. The second half of the nineteenth century was a period of accelerated industrial development. Coal mines and

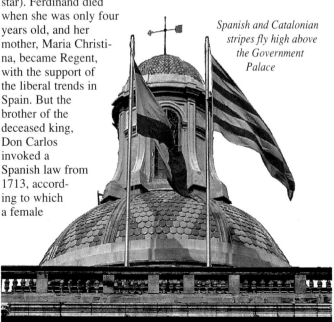

Spanish and Catalonian stripes fly high above the Government Palace

Cannons used in battles, now on exhibition at the Military Museum

various metals found in Catalonia were exploited for building machinery for factories and for heating steam boilers; the cotton industry prospered. By virtue of its economic status and power, Barcelona hosted the Grand International Fair in 1888.

Masses of wretched workers streamed to Barcelona, concentrating in the impoverished outskirts. They were fruitful soil for the rise of socialistic and anarchistic organizations. Concurrently, in Catalonia, separatism and the aspiration for autonomy increased. One of the key figures in the movements which demanded self-government was the renowned Catalan poet Joan Maragall.

These conflicting currents found violent expression: first, in 1909, when an anarchist revolt broke out in Barcelona,

following the mobilization of a large number of soldiers, especially from the poorer classes, to fight in Morocco. The uprising spread from Barcelona to other cities in Catalonia. The army, which had begun to emerge as a political force, clearly supporting the right-wing elements, arrived in the region to restore order, led by General Weyler.

The seven days which ensued in July of that year entered the Spanish history books as the "Tragic Week" *Setmana Tragica*. The suppression of the uprising involved much bloodshed and property damage. Monasteries were burnt, and priests murdered: on the other end of the political spectrum, the army slaughtered rebel activists.

In 1914, Catalonia achieved a certain amount of autonomy, but separatist leaders demanded full self-government. In 1917, after strikes by the workers, disturbances broke out once more, and the army was again called in to suppress the rebels with an iron fist. And, precisely during this difficult period of struggle, Barcelona again experienced a period of economic prosperity. This was brought about by the First World War which was then in full sway in Europe, though Spain remained neutral. The city's port became a teeming crossroads to the warring nations. Great profits flowed into the armored vaults of the owners of the shipping companies and to industrial plants in Barcelona and throughout Catalonia. At the same time, nationalist political agitation led to the establishment of a Catalonian parliament in Barcelona (1918) – the *Mancommunidad de Catalunya*.

After the war, the social pendulum swung back, and the city was again swept by social ferment, followed by riots stirred up by the leftist anarchist and socialist movements. Violent confrontations occurred between local civil government authorities and the army. In 1922 in Catalonia, a broad movement was organized which demanded that Spain become a federation of states, as a condition for Catalonia remaining in the political framework of Spain. One year later, a common front of Catalonian and Basque nationalists was organized.

Against this background, in 1923, with the support of the army and the king, General Primo de Rivera seized power and turned Spain into a totalitarian country.

All political activity was banned, the legislative body was disbanded, and the government was organized on the model of the Italian fascist regime. In Barcelona, hate for the dictator was intense, all the more so, since all Catalonia's privileges of self-government had been revoked, and the *Mancommunidad* had been immediately dismissed. However, the government of de Rivera collapsed when in 1930, after the great economic depression and the plunge in the value of the Spanish currency, he was forced to resign and leave the country.

The Exhibition Towers, built for the "International Exhibition of 1929"

Rule passed to General Dámaso Berenguer, who in the "Pact of San Sebastián", concluded with the socialists, liberal and conservative groups and the Catalonian movements, committed himself to establishing a republic in Spain. In the framework of this agreement, Catalonia won its autonomy, led by Francesc Macia, and Barcelona became the capital of the Catalonian sub-republic.

In mid-1931, elections for local governments were held in Spain. From partial results, it became clear that the candidates of the "Pact of San Sebastián" had won, but the final results were never published. The reason was that when the preliminary information became known, King Alfonso XIII had already left Spain, without announcing his resignation. In Madrid on April 14th a revolutionary assembly of republican representatives took over the government.

In the general elections which took place afterwards, the left won an overwhelming majority of the seats in the Spanish legislature (Cortes). The constitution proclaimed the elimination of titles of nobility, accepted regional autonomous government, and set aside the extra privileges of the Catholic church and its status as the official state religion. In a plebiscite, Catalonia accepted the "Catalan Autonomy Statute", and an independent government (Generalitat) was set up, having wide-ranging authority. But the economic recession and the severe continuing industrial crisis put a damper on expectations. The Left found itself under attack by the anarchists and by the Right, at the same time. The situation deteriorated. Frequent strikes, political murders, the burning of monasteries and churches, and the damaging of private property became daily occurrences. An internal earthquake was only a matter of time.

On July 17, 1936 the revolt broke out. The Spanish army in Morocco, led by General Franco, raised the banner of revolt against the government and, in a matter of days, all of Spain was ablaze. Still, the government did not

fall. In Barcelona, soldiers managed to gain control over their rebelling officers and disarm them, proclaiming their loyalty to the Republican government. The Nationalist soldier, General Goded, who was sent to seize control in Barcelona was captured by government loyalists and put to death. The revolution failed, and a cruel civil war began, which, during the following two years and eight months, was to bleed Spain unmercifully. The rebels, who called themselves "Nationalists", were in control of a large part of the well-organized, well-trained army, supported by the rightist movements, the fascists and the royalists. They organized the *unta* for national defense and chose Franco as *Caudillo* – head of state. Opposing them were the Republicans, a very diverse and divided camp. The socialists, the communists, the anarchists, and others, each pulled in a different direction.

Spain became a battlefield in which various European political forces took part, either directly or indirectly. Nazi Germany and Fascist Italy aided the Nationalists, while the Soviet Union, the socialist government in France, and leftist volunteers from throughout the world supported the Republicans. The struggle assumed a worldwide character of a fight between totalitarianism and democracy. The Nationalists had the upper hand, both militarily, in the

fierce battles, and in their more unified stand. Conflicts within the Socialist party and street battles between government supporters and anarchists caused crisis after crisis and weakened the government stand. The Republican government suffered defeats, and at the end of October 1937, it was forced to retreat to Barcelona, the main base of its support. The difficult situation on the battlefield, the crowded conditions of the masses of refugees who came seeking shelter in the city, the Nationalist shellings, and the arguments which broke out between members of the central government and members of the local Catalonian government, all increased the despair. But the war continued, with more and more bloodshed. In December of 1938, the forces of General Franco, who had refused Republican peace offers and insisted on unconditional surrender, took the offensive with an all-out attack on Catalonia. In January 1939, wounded, exhausted, its streets filled with masses of hungry refugees, Barcelona fell to the Nationalists. Two months later, the civil war ended, with the total victory of General Franco.

Spain paid a heavy price in blood – more than 500,000 people were killed in battle. Franco's followers executed almost all the Republican officers who fell into their hands, thousands of soldiers were arrested, and more than 300,000 refugees fled the country. At the beginning of his totalitarian rule, the dictator Franco abrogated all rights of Catalonian self-government. All political activity was forbidden, and activists were thrown into prison. The local language and culture were suppressed, and publication of newspapers and books in the Catalonian language was strictly forbidden. The president of the autonomous government of Catalonia, Lluís Companys, was executed by a firing squad in 1940. Other leaders fled and spent the remainder of their lives far from their homeland, among the approximately 100,000 Catalonian expatriates.

The 1954 constitution proclaimed Spain to be a monarchy without a king, with Franco as its regent. The general chose Juan Carlos, the grandson of Alfonso XIII, to be the king-designate. Once again, in contrast to the difficult internal political circumstances, the economic situation improved. Contributory factors included the fact that Spain had not taken part in the Second World War, the economic technocracy which Franco had established, industrial modernization and, of course, the growth of European tourism after the Cold War subsided. Spain was able to break out of its political isolation, to sign agreements establishing American military bases on its territory, in return for financial aid, and even, in 1955, to join the United Nations. In 1970, preliminary contacts were made with the European Common Market.

In 1975, General Franco died, and Juan Carlos I ascended to the throne. Because of his personal liberal outlook and his wise and correct assessment of the world scene, and, particularly, the European political map, the king unequivocally proclaimed the country to be a parliamentary democracy, to the disappointment of traditional Spanish rightists. He allowed political parties to be active, and two years later, in

Flags at the Olympic Village

Barcelona is located between the Mediterranean coast and the hills of the Sierra de Collserola range

1977, free general elections were held in Spain, which made democracy a reality. The "Spanish miracle" became an actuality and, in 1986, Spain became a full member of the European Common Market. Previously, in 1979, following a decision of the Spanish legislature, Catalonia (along with Navarre, the land of the Basques, and Galicia) again became autonomous, and the Catalonian language was officially recognized. The king took the important symbolic step of visiting Barcelona which, once more, took its place as the regional capital. On that occasion, he delivered his speech to the people in the Catalan language.

On October 17, 1986, Barcelona was declared an Olympic city. It was chosen to host the Twenty-Fifth Olympic Games in 1992. The two short weeks of the games contributed immensely to the growth and progress of the city's transport, communications, tourism and public services.

Geography

Barcelona is the capital of the district of Catalonia and serves as an important cultural and commercial center for Catalonians as well as for all Spaniards. It has the reputation of being a more "European" city than other Spanish cities, both because of the character of its inhabitants and because of its cosmopolitan atmosphere. It is the second largest city in the country (after Madrid), and has the largest port.

Barcelona is located

The Generalitat – the district government

crossroads for the traveller going from Madrid to the French Riviera and serves as a starting point for sailing to Palma de Mallorca.

About 1,800,000 people live in Barcelona. The population of greater Barcelona (the city and the surrounding environs) is estimated at about 4,000,000. Population density is about 17,200 per sq/km. It is one of the five most densely populated cities in the world (in this respect, it is akin to Tokyo, Mexico City, etc.). About two thirds of the inhabitants of Barcelona are Catalans. The large majority are practicing Catholics.

northeast of Spain, between the Mediterranean coast and the green hills of the Sierra de Collserola range. The city extends over less than 100 sq/kms and is mostly flat. It is bounded by the Riu Besos River on the south and the Riu Liobregat River on the north. The new city is built with straight, wide, long streets which crisscross in a precise pattern: while in the surrounding suburbs, which were originally villages, the streets are short and winding, as in the old city.

Barcelona is located 613 kms from Madrid, 1092 kms from Paris, and only 149 kms south of the town of La Jonquera, on the French border. It is the

CLIMATE

Barcelona enjoys a temperate, pleasant Mediterranean climate. During the winter months of December to February the average temperature is 9-10° Celsius. The average rainfall in the winter months in Barcelona resembles that of any other Mediterranean city and does not constitute a hindrance for tourists during that season.

In autumn and spring, the days are usually sunny and pleasant, and these are the most suitable seasons to visit Barcelona. In spring (from the end of March until May) and in autumn (from the end of September until the beginning of November), the average temperature rises to between 14-19° Celsius. Summers are dry, and the temperature rises to between 23-26° Celsius on an average. Only on rare occasions does the temperature ever drop below zero in winter or rise above 34° in summer.

The annual rainfall comes to 600 mm, and both locals and visitors take pleasure in the more than 2,500 yearly hours of sunshine.

Government

Barcelona is the capital of the Catalonian district, which enjoys a certain degree of autonomy within the Spanish political framework. The district government (the Generalitat) is elected by its six million inhabitants. It administers the daily life of the region by virtue of the taxes collected by the central government in Spain. For the stranger making a short visit to Barcelona, this fact may have no immediate, practical significance, but for the local population, which fought so long to gain its independence and to retain its unique identity, this autonomy is the source of national joy and pride.

Economy

The district of Catalonia, and the capital Barcelona in particular, enjoy commercial and economic prosperity, and are taking the lead in enabling Spain to become a first-rank economic power in Europe. The district of Catalonia is the richest and most industrialized region in all of Spain and produces over 20% of the total national product – even though it has only about 6,000,000 inhabitants (less than 15% of the total number of inhabitants in the country).

About forty four percent of Barcelona's inhabitants are

industrial workers. The main branch is the textile industry. The city manufactures over two thirds of the entire national production in this branch. Other outstanding industries include: highly developed chemical concerns, paper production, plastics, leather goods, wines, fruits, and agricultural machinery. In commerce, the stock market is the second largest in Spain, and it conducts about one quarter of all the trade in the Spanish market. Barcelona also has a well-developed commercial port, one of the most advanced in Europe, which is an important factor in the city's economy.

The Sacred Family Church – Gaudí's largest architectural wonder, today still remains unfinished

As a result of the entrance of Spain into the European Community, many giant firms throughout the world began to show an interest in the Spanish economy. These companies – from all over Europe, Japan, and the United States, started to invest in developing Spanish industry, placing the emphasis on the Catalonian region. Cognizant of the commercial-industrial potential of the region, these firms embarked on large investment projects in Barcelona and the surrounding area.

Most of these investments were in Barcelona's traditional economic spheres: mechanization, textiles, chemicals, etc. In their wake, Barcelona began to resume its place as Spain's leading city, economically.

The acceleration of economic activity in Barcelona and its environs has changed its economic character and the way of life of its inhabitants. On the one hand, many more employment opportunities have been created in all spheres of industry. At the same time, there has been an increase in the number of tourists who include a visit to Catalonia in their trip to Spain. On the other hand, the city's leaders have encountered a new problem – an increase in imports to the area which has caused inflation.

The 1992 Olympic Games, which were held in Barcelona,

At the Picasso Museum

gave new impetus to the city's growth and brought about a wave of prosperity unparalled in earlier times.

Culture and Art

Barcelona is distinguished by its open atmosphere (the result of the intermingling of many different cultures), its economic strength, its location at the crossroads of commerce and shipping, and its aspirations for independence. These have been the source of artistic and cultural ferment which has filled the city's history with the names of internationally famous artists, many of the first rank.

One of the most outstanding and important of the city's artists is **Antoni Gaudí**. Architect and sculptor, Gaudí worked in the city at the beginning of the twentieth century, constructing modern buildings which are still considered to be most advanced even now at the end of the century. The surrealist painter, **Joan Miró** was born in Barcelona in 1893. He was much influenced by the atmosphere in the city and the art styles he found there. When he was 25 years old, he moved to Paris, but still considered Barcelona his home. In 1974, he established a museum in his home in Barcelona, where most of his works were housed. **Picasso**, too, began his painting career in Barcelona and, before his death, sent many of his works here. Today, these paintings are housed in the museum which bears his name.

LITERATURE

Literature, being always an important factor of the original Catalonian culture, had an extraordinary renaissance at the beginning of the 19th century, with works of such writers as Rubió y Ors and Balaguer, the author of the *History of Catalonia* (1863). This phenomenon reached its climax at the end of the century, with Angel Guiverá, the talented playwright and the two great poets – Jacint Verdaguer i Santaló (author of the well known epic poem *Atlántida*) and the Barcelonian Joan Maragall, one of the main figures of Catalonian culture.

The chimneys of Casa Milà are an example of Gaudí's dynamic style

ARCHITECTURE

A visit to Barcelona is an architectural experience of the first order, and many young architects come to the city in order to study its great builders. The combination of a port city open to varied influences, the pleasant weather, and the relative economic well-being in the city throughout most of its history, was, apparently, the reason for the development of its architecture and the integration of new ideas in it. The Museum of Art of Catalonia (MAC), located in the Palau Nacional in Montjuïc, houses many remains from the various styles which flourished in the city and is one of the world's leading museums in the field of architecture.

The first impressive remains we encounter are from the **Romanesque** period. This style reached the area at the end of the eleventh century and was adopted by the noblemen of the city, who popularized it throughout Catalonia. The Romanesque style developed in Western Europe and is built on the simple, stark lines of stone structures (mostly castles and churches) with sloping roofs. Outstanding Romanesque buildings in Barcelona include the Benedictine Church Sant Paul del Camp and the Capella de Santa Llucia in the city's cathedral.

The next period which left its clear mark on the city was the **Gothic** period, which dominated Europe between the thirteenth and fifteenth centuries, replacing the Romanesque period. Gothic architecture is characterized by its pointed arches, its extensive embellishments, its columns and porticos which result in a change in the perception of space. Such buildings glorified the name of the king and of God and diminished to a minimum the stature of man in the temple. The transition from Romanesque to Gothic architecture in Barcelona occurred toward the end of the twelfth century and the beginning of the thirteenth. Influenced by the Mediterranean spirit, a Gothic-Catalonian style of architecture evolved in the city. The local architects preferred width to height, insisting upon human scale and proportions, etc.

Barcelona boasts a marvelous Gothic Quarter in the center of the city, which still serves as a living model of the wonders of the Gothic style and is a central focus of interest. Among the outstanding buildings in the quarter are the grand cathedral, the Palace of the Generalitat, the Santa Maria del Mar Church, the Maritime Museum in the Royal Shipyards, and others.

The third style which dominates the landscape of Barcelona, and, perhaps the most famous of all, is **modernism**, which appeared in the city about one hundred

years ago, and has managed, in the course of the last thirty years, to confound accepted conventions in the world of

architecture. The leading figures of this architectural renaissance were Doménec y Montaner, Puig y Cadafalch, Ricardo Botill, and, above all, the famous Antoni Gaudí, who created his own original modernistic style. The modernistic style challenged the rigid perceptions of architecture, bringing flow and color to its buildings. The modernists broke the straight and symmetric lines and initiated the use of colorful and pliable new materials inside the buildings, thus creating startling and exciting forms and effects.

Outstanding in the modernist

movement is the genius of Gaudí who built those structures which are the leading examples of this new architectonic style, in the city. Masterpieces, such as La Pedrera, Parc Güell, and, above all, the Sagrada Familia Church – whose construction commenced in 1884 and is still going on at present – leave the viewer in awe.

Gaudí and his colleagues were geniuses who came before their time. Construction prevailing in Europe and throughout the world tends to be industrial, block-shaped, and grey, but the splashes of color and joy which the modernists introduced to Barcelona provide a ray of hope and give promise of other possibilities.

BULLFIGHTS

The bullfight, or *corrida* as it is referred to by the Spaniards, is the most famous Spanish fiesta. The name of Spain, in our imaginations, has always been linked with bullfights

involving a festively attired matador putting a large wild black bull through its paces.

For the Spaniards, bullfighting is the national sport. They consider the corrida to be a true art, combining elements of beauty and nobility with elements of strength and cruelty. The origin of the art of bullfighting (*tauromaquia*) is very ancient. It was already known thousands of years ago. In Crete, for example, it was practiced as early as the 2nd millenium BC, but the way it is practiced today evolved about 200 years ago.

The corrida has clear and fixed rules which include several stages: first is the ceremony of dressing the bullfighter – who is mistakenly referred to as a *matador* but should really be called a *torero*. Dressing the bullfighter is important in itself and takes place before a small, select audience in the bullfighter's room. The garb of the torero sparkles, is colorful, and very tight-fitting. On his head is a black hat, and on his back hangs a braid which will be cut on the day he retires from the bullring.

After the dressing stage comes the prayer ceremony. The bullfighter prays to his special saints, including in his prayer magic and religious elements which are related to the bullfight itself.

After the prayer, the torero goes into the arena, and over his arm is draped a cape of embroidered silk.

Following a ceremony

accompanied by an orchestra playing the *pasodoble*, one of the apprentice youths opens the door where the bull is being held. When the door opens, the bull charges forth wildly, and the orchestral drums herald his entrance into the arena. The apprentices then try to draw the attention of the bull in order to give the bullfighter an opportunity to assess him.

While the torero is changing his cape, the orchestral fanfare signals the appearance of the spear-bearers (*picadores*). The prick of the spears in the bull's back draws his blood and tires him but also makes him wilder.

At this point, the star of the show, the torero is left alone in the arena, with the red cloth and the angry bull. Even those who have misgivings about the cruelty which has dominated the corrida up to this stage can appreciate the elegance with which the torero teases the bull, his swift, clean movements, and the courage he demonstrates. The audience responds to the torero's more successful maneuvers with cries of "*Olé!*"

When the torero feels that the bull is exhausted, he tries to thrust the sword into the back of the bull. The object is to kill the bull with one sword thrust (thus also ending the suffering of the tortured animal).

In reward for a successful fight, the bullfighter is given the ear and tail of the bull.

Bullfighting – a controversial pastime

Not all Spaniards agree about the bullfights. Among the inveterate devotees of this sport, there are many who would prefer not to have such events take place or even to forbid them. Opponents of these fights oppose them on two counts – the real danger to the torero, as well as the cruel torture of the helpless bull.

The famous bullfights take place in the grand bullring at the Plaça de Toros Monumental at 743 Gran Vía de las Corts Catalanes. The season for corridas in Barcelona is between March and September, usually on Thursday, Sunday and holidays. The main ticket office is located at 24 Muntaner Street (Tel. 253-3821). Any unsold tickets will be offered for sale at the stadium one hour before the performance, which usually begins at 5:30pm. The entrance fee varies according to rows and their situation – in the shade (*sombra*) or in the sun (*sol*).

If the aura of the arena strikes your fancy, or if you grew up on the tales of Ernest Hemingway, don't miss the *Bar del toreros*. This is a restaurant entirely devoted to bulls and bullfighters, a place with a past and a great deal of atmosphere. It is located in a small lane at 5 Carrer d'en Xucla, behind the Church of Betlem in Rambla Boulevard.

PART TWO – SETTING OUT

When To Come

The hot summer months (June to August) are the height of the tourist season. At that time, the city loses some of its charm, for it is filled with a stream of visitors from many lands, speaking a jumble of languages. Prices, too, jump skyhigh at this time. Hotel reservations must be made well in advance. The seasons recommended for visiting the city are autumn – from the end of September until the middle of November – and spring – from the end of March until the middle of May. During these seasons, temperatures are comfortable, sports and artistic events in the city are in full swing, and the small number of tourists means that every place is less crowded and prices are lower. It should be noted that even those arriving in Barcelona in the winter can enjoy their stay here, because of the city's temperate climate.

Holidays and Celebrations

In addition to Sundays, the following holidays and special events are celebrated in Barcelona:

January 1 – New Year's Day and the beginning of the "Three Kings Festival". Christian mythology tells of three kings who came from the east, and on the way, the place of Jesus' birth was revealed to them. Children write letters to the "three kings", and go down to the harbor to see them arrive from the east. During the festival, children are given dolls and traditional sweets. On January 5, the children leave a shoe on the porch, and the following morning, they find it full of goodies, brought by the kings.

January 6 – Epiphany is celebrated, along with the end of the "Three Kings" festival.

February – Carnestoltes, the

At the Cathedral during the Holy Week celebrations

Traditional celebrations in Barcelona

traditional carnival, also celebrated in Venice, Brazil, and elsewhere. These celebrations are not grandiose in Barcelona. For festive processions and masks, you can go to nearby Sitges (see the chapter "Excursions"). The date varies.

March 19 – San José: a local Barcelona holiday.

March-April – Easter: Holy Week celebrations (Semana Santa). During this week, many shops and restaurants are closed. Banks are closed on Fri.-Sat.-Sun.-Mon. of the Easter week.

April 23 – Festa de Sant Jordi, the holiday of Saint Jordi, the patron saint of Catalonia. A holiday when gifts are exchanged and the Generalitat Palace is open to the public for visits. An especially popular

holiday, also known as "Pascua Granada".

May 1 – workers' holiday.

May 15 – Pentecost. Religious processions.

June 24 – Sant Joan's day. Celebrations begin on the eve of this day and culminate in the Verbena celebrations on Montjuïc Hill, accompanied by fireworks. A special food is eaten on this holiday: Coca de Sant Joan, a sweet pastry with sugared fruits and nuts.

August 15 – celebration of the Assumption.

September 11 – Diada, the national day of Catalonia, commemorating the conquest of the city on this day by King Philip V of Spain in the year 1700. A day of memorial ceremonies and political gatherings.

September 24 – La Merce, Barcelona's saint, is celebrated in a very popular holiday, with religious processions, sports competitions, Sardana dancing, fireworks, etc. Celebrations begin on this date and continue for about a week and include musical and dramatic performances and even mock battles in the streets and in the squares.

October 12 – Festa de la Hispanitat. National holiday of Spain.

November 1 – All Saints' Day. Celebrated by family gatherings.

December 6 – Dia de la Constitució. Spanish Constitution Day.

December 8 – La Inmaculada Concepció.

December 13 – Santa Lucia's Day. Crab fair next to the cathedral and opening of the city's musical season.

December 25 – Christmas.

December 26 – Sant Esteve.

How Long to Stay

It is possible to see all the tourist sites in the city in one or two days, but the pace would be very fast and very tiring. We recommend a stay of at least four days for a sense of Barcelona's atmosphere and uniqueness. Of course, the longer the visit, the better.

In addition to Barcelona, it is worth devoting one or two days to the beautiful sites nearby. Either stay overnight or return to Barcelona in the evening after your day of sight-seeing (see "Excursions").

Documents and Customs

Citizens of the European Community, West European countries, the United States and Canada only need a passport to enter Spain for a period of up to six months. Others need a visa, which must be requested in advance from the Spanish Embassy nearest to your place of residence.

Those wanting to extend their stay beyond the period permitted in their visitor's visa should apply to the Spanish immigration department at 16 Via Laietana, second floor (Tel. 310-000). Open Mon.-Thurs. 9:30am-12:30pm. Bring three photos, your valid passport, the return ticket, and the equivalent of $20 (for one-two entries), or $40 (for three entries). The

You do not need an international driver's license if you come from Western Europe or North America. An ordinary driver's license from these countries is sufficient for driving in Spain.

An international student card will entitle you to price reductions in a number of places and to free entrance to many museums, so it is worth bringing this card if you are entitled to it.

Insurance: Don't leave home without sufficient health insurance to cover expenses for a doctor or a hospital in time of need. In addition to health insurance, it is worth insuring your possessions, so that you will get your money back in case your luggage is damaged or lost.

visa will be given later the same day.

Customs regulations allow you to bring in your personal effects, as in most places throughout the world. You can also bring two cameras and ten rolls of film. Most of the customs officials do not make an issue about this, but if you are bringing several cameras (for your personal use), you should contact the nearest Spanish Embassy for a special permit in order to avoid unpleasantness upon entering the country. There is no limitation on the amount of money you are allowed to bring in to the country, but you are not permitted to take out more than 1,000,000 pesetas in local currency or more than the equivalent of $8,000 in foreign currency.

How Much does it Cost

A visit to Spain in general and to Barcelona, in particular, is not at all inexpensive. A double room in a 3-star hotel costs about $100-120. A meal in a good, but not luxurious, restaurant costs about $35 per person. A medium-priced trip would cost about $240 for a couple for one day or about $150 for a single person. Tourists interested in a higher standard would need to spend at least $240 or more per person per day.

Young backpackers can manage on $25 a day, which will buy them a bed in a hostel, cheap meals, and the chance to wear out the soles of their shoes on the city's sidewalks.

What to Wear

During the summer, don't forget light airy clothing. You also need bathing suits and hats if you want to spend time at one of the lovely beaches near the city. During a Mediterranean winter, you don't need a fur coat or ski equipment. A warm jacket and heavy socks will suffice.

A neat pleasant appearance is much appreciated by the local population, but there is no need to exaggerate about formal attire for restaurants or cultural performances, since this is not required in the large majority of cases. Light sporty clothing, appropriate for the summer, plus a warm jacket and a scarf in the winter, will meet most of your needs.

PART THREE – EASING THE SHOCK: WHERE HAVE WE LANDED?

How to Get There

BY AIR

The international airport of Barcelona, El Part, is located twelve kms west of the city. It has been renovated in preparation for the Olympic Games, to facilitate the reception of the incoming passengers. The *Iberia* airline has a permanent *Air Shuttle* between Barcelona and Madrid from 6:30am-10:30pm. *Aviaco* (Tel. 478-2411) offers national flights. *Viva Air* (Tel. 478-6266) links Barcelona with Palma de Mallorca. Both companies belong to the *Iberia Group. Iberia*, *Air France*, *Alitalia*, *British Airways*, *Swissair*, *KLM*, *Lufthansa*, *Sabena*, and *TWA* all offer daily flights from Barcelona to the home destinations of these airlines (in summer, sometimes more than once a day).

There is a bank in the terminal building which is open continuously between 7am-11pm. On Saturdays and Sundays, passengers can use the bank branch in the outer arrival terminal, after passing through customs. If the official isn't there, knock on the glass and wait for him.

In the outer terminal there is also a tourist bureau, but the

A view from within Estació de França

information it has to offer is very limited. At the pavillion of the local hoteliers association you can reserve a room in the city. Car rental firms, *Hertz* (Tel. 370-5811), *Avis* (Tel. 379-4026), *Europcar* (Tel. 478-3178) and others also have representatives in the outer terminal.

Helicopter services: *Taf Helicópters*, Tel. 209-2755, fax 201-3002; *Gestair*, Tel. 478-0722, fax 478-0911.

FROM THE AIRPORT TO BARCELONA

From the airport it is possible to reach the center of town by taxi, by train or by bus. The train connection to Plaça de Catalunya in the city center is excellent. From the air terminal, a train leaves every thirty minutes, starting at 6:30am; the last train leaves the airport at 10:40pm. *Aerobús*, a new bus shuttle service, run by the *Transports Ciutat Comtal* company, links the city with the airport. The buses leave from the Plaça de Catalunya and the airport every fifteen minutes on weekdays, and every thirty minutes during weekends and holidays. The *EA* line connects the airport with downtown Barcelona every 80 minutes – from 7am-8:20pm (Barcelona-Airport) and from 6:20am-7:40pm (Airport-Barcelona).

BY TRAIN

Those coming by train will arrive at the Barcelona Sants Central Station (Estació Sants-Central) at the Plaça Païso Catalans or at the modern refurbished Estació de França station (referred to by the locals as Término). The railroad information service provides detailed information at the Sants Station (Tel. 490-0202). From the train stations, there is a direct connection by subway to all parts of the city. These train stations, both the modern and the older one, are near the Plaça d'Espanya in the center of the city.

The train trip from Paris to Barcelona takes about 12 hours, from Geneva also about 12 hours. From Marseille, the trip takes about 8 hours. Inside Spain there is a good connection between Barcelona and Madrid (8 hours), Saragossa (4.5 hours), Valencia (5 hours), and other Spanish cities.

Passengers under 26 years of age, receive large reductions. Other reductions are offered on return train tickets to pensioners, etc. *Eurail Pass* tickets entitle the holders to free travel in Spain. The Spanish Railroad Authority *Renfe* (Tel. 490-0202) offers a *Tourist Card* which entitles the holder to free travel within the borders of the country (except for the International Fast Trains *Talgo and Eurocity*).

Reductions are also offered to young people and pensioners. These tickets may be purchased in the Sants station, where information is available.

BY BUS

The *Julia* company provides regular bus service between Barcelona and other cities throughout Europe, such as Lisbon, London, Paris, Rome, Munich, etc. More information is available at the office of the company: 12 Plaça Universitat (Tel. 490-4000). The *Via Euro-lines* company, whose office is located at 117 Pau Claris (Tel. 317-3346) operates buses to Amsterdam and Paris. You can reach Rome, London, Holland, etc. with the *Berbus* company (Tel. 329-6406).

Bus tickets cost about the same as train tickets, but the trip takes longer and is more tiring, so it is preferable to take the train and use the bus for short trips of only a few hours to sites near the city.

The *Sarfa* company (Estació d'Autobusos Barcelona Nord, 80 Ali-bei, Tel. 265-1158) operates an efficient line from Barcelona to the popular Costa Brava beaches. You can reach Montserrat with the *Julia* company, mentioned above. The *Renfe* Rail Authority also operates buses to Madrid and other cities in Spain from the Norte-Vilanova station next to the Arc del Triomf. You can

At the city Port

find out more details about schedules and prices from *Renfe* information at Tel. 490-0202.

ORGANIZED HITCH-HIKING
If you drive a car and have empty places, or if you want to join such a trip, you can apply to two agencies in the city which coordinate passengers with drivers and vice versa (for a fee for the driver and the agency). The fee is not high, and this is the cheapest way to travel, except for hitch-hiking, of course. The agencies are:

Barnastop: 29 Sant Ramón, Tel. 443-0832. Mon.-Fri. 11am-2pm and 5-7pm.
Comparco: 31 Ribes, Tel. 443-0632.

These offices are not open in winter. They operate mostly between April to October.

BY SEA
Even though Barcelona has a large port, not many ships carry passengers. Most of the sea traffic is found on the ferries to the Balearic Islands. The *Transmediterránea* company operates trips from Barcelona port to Palma de Mallorca, Ibiza, Mahón. The trip takes about 8-9 hours. For details, contact the company office at 6-8 Av. Drassanes, Tel. 317-6311.

The Marina Port Vell (Varadero s/n, 08003 Barcelona, Tel. 484-2300,

fax 484-2333) provides a very convenient mooring for medium and large sized yachts. It also offers a wide range of ship-handling services, restaurants, etc.

BY CAR
Road A-17 connects Barcelona with the French border point at the town of La Jonquera. Road A-2 leads from Barcelona to the interior of the country – to Saragossa and Madrid, while the main coastal highway A-7 leads south to Valencia. There is a toll for the use of these main road arteries. You can avoid paying the toll by using internal roads to reach and leave the city.

The top speed limit on the expressways is 120 km/h, and within the city, only 60km/h. Drivers from Common Market countries do not need an international driver's license or any special insurance, but it is worth getting a "Green Card" (International Insurance Certificate). This card serves as an insurance certificate for car towing, and we recommend it. Drivers who are not citizens of the Common Market countries should contact the nearest Spanish Consulate and clarify the Spanish legal requirements for drivers' licenses, vehicles, and insurance before entering the country to avoid unpleasant surprises at the border crossings.

Urban Transportation

Transportation inside the city is well-developed, efficient, and cheap, it is unnecessary to hire cars inside the crowded city and waste time looking for a safe parking space. In addition to the many taxis, you can exploit the subway and the convenient buses, or you can take advantage of the compactness of the city and that old reliable means of transportation, your feet. More information about local public transportation is available at Tel. 412-0000.

SUBWAY
The excellent local subway has four lines: L1 (marked in red), L3 (green), L4 (yellow), L5 (blue). The Generalitat Government operates two additional lines – one to Tibidabo Hill and the other to the western part of the city. These six lines connect at many points, making a convenient network for getting easily from one place to another. When you want to go to a particular spot, use the map that is available in every subway station to clarify which station is closest to your destination.

The subway operates Mon.-Thurs. from 5am-11pm; on Fri., Sat., and holidays' eves from 5am-1am, and on Sun. from 6am-11pm.

You can reduce the price of a trip considerably by using multi-trip tickets. The T1 ticket is valid for 10 trips on the urban subway, on buses, on the local trains of the Generalitat and on the cable car to Muntjuïc Hill. It includes a 40% reduction. For an additional reduction, you can buy the T2 ticket, which is valid for all the above mentioned transport, except buses. The tickets are not limited to the personal use of the purchaser, and a number of people travelling together can use the same ticket. Such tickets may be purchased at subway stations, bus stations and from automatic dispensers.

During the summer season, another type of ticket is also available, which is valid for all types of urban transportation for one day.

BUSES
Urban buses operate between

6:30am-10pm daily, and the important lines also offer nightime service until 4pm.

You will find a colored code on the bus which will help you identify its route:

Red – This bus passes through the center of the city (near Plaça de Catalunya).

Blue – This bus operates even at night, passing through the center of the city.

Yellow – This bus crosses the city, but not via the center.

Green – Buses on this line go to the city's periphery.

Bus travel is very comfortable and pleasant. The buses are not full (most people travel by subway), their markings are clear and easily identifiable, and they are reasonably frequent.

TAXIS

The taxis, which are painted black and yellow, are not hard to stop on the street. All taxis are equipped with meters. In addition to the regular fare, the driver will charge an additional sum for each hour that he needs to wait and will also charge extra to enter the airport or the railroad station, as well as for each large suitcase or pet which you bring along. About 1,000 of the 11,000 taxis accept credit cards.

The local taxi drivers are known for their impatience and impoliteness, so you should prepare the name of your desired destination in advance and in writing. You may find that your cab driver (like most of them) speaks only Spanish.

Barnataxi, Tel. 357-7755.
Taxi Radio Móvil, Tel. 358-1111.

The "Blue Tram"

Teletaxi, Tel. 392-2222.
Radio Taxi Expres, Tel.
490-2222
Metropolitana, Tel. 300-3811
Mens, Tel. 387-1000.

Those wishing to travel
by horse and carriage,
can call Tel. 421-8804
or 421-1549.

CABLE CAR AND FUNICULAR

In the elevated sections of the
city, special means of transportation have been set up,
which serve both to convey
people to their destinations
and, at the same time, are
tourist attractions in themselves.

The cablecar (*Telefèric*)
operates on Montjuïc Hill
(near the station of line 61).
This cablecar can be reached
via the *Funicular* from the
Paral-lel subway station
(line L3). Another line
operates from the same hill
to the port but is not
recommended for those who
suffer from fear of heights.

Other *Funicular* lines connect
train stations of the Generalitat
in the Av. del Tibidabo and the
Peu del Funicular with the
lovely observation points on
the hill.

The Blue Tram (Tramvia Blau)
– a single short line connects
the Av. del Tibidado station to
the beginning of the ascent to
Tibidado Hill by funicular.

CAR RENTAL

Hertz: 8-10 Tuset, Tel.
217-3248.
Avis: 209 Casanova, Tel.
209-9533; 487-8754.
Budget: 15 Av. Roma, Tel.
322-9012.

Slowly ascend this magnificent staircase to feel the grand atmosphere at the Palace Hotel

Europcar: 214 Viladomat, Tel. 439-8403.
Atesa: 141 Balmes, Tel. 237-8140.
Vanguard: 31 Londres, Tel. 439-3880.
Tot Car: 91-95 Josep Tarradellas, Tel. 405-3433.
Rental auto: 32 Av. Sarriá, Tel. 430-9071.
Regente: 382 Aragó, Tel. 487-9589.
Ital: 71 Trav. Gràcia, Tel. 201-2199.
Docar: 18 Montengre, Tel. 322-9008.
Gestvi: 12 Gran Vía Charles III, Tel. 490-9763.

Limousine Rental: 13 San José, Tel. 473-6710.

Motorcycles for hire:
Vanguard, 31 Londres St., Tel. 239-3880.

Accommodation

Barcelona is renowned for its hospitality. Miguel de Cervantes, author of *Don Quixote* praised the good qualities of the city's innkeepers. Most of the city's hoteliers are friendly, honest, and speak foreign languages such as English, French, and German. The local hotels are classified by letters into different categories. H stands for Hotel, HS stands for a lower-class hotel (*hostal*), P means a pension (*pensio*), and CH is a guesthouse (*casa d' hostes*).

Beside the letter signifying the type of accommodation is the number of stars designating the grade of the place on a scale of one to five stars. It should be noted that the hotels in Barcelona are at a lower grade than those usually found in other western European countries (despite the high prices). The system of assigning stars to indicate the level of service is misleading for many tourists since here, the rating is high in comparison to the service offered.

Most hotels were modernized and upgraded in preparation for the 1992 Olympics. Since the city is so densely populated, most of the hotels are located close to the main points of interest.

Expensive hotels in Barcelona

will cost anywhere from $220 for a single person and from $240 for a couple for one night. Moderately priced hotels range from $120-$220 for a single person and $150-$240 for a couple per night. Modest hotels charge between $50-$120 for a single person and $75-$150 for a couple. In regular hostels and inexpensive pensions, single and double rooms cost $20 and up; in youth hostels the rate is even lower.

LUXURY HOTELS

Princesa Sofía: 4 Pl. Papa Pius XII, Tel. 330-7111, fax 330-7621. Modern building, an excellent hotel, one of the most prestigious in the city as well as the largest.

Hotel Claris: 150 Pau Claris. Situated at the center of Barcelona. One of the city's flagship hotels. Tel. 487-6262. fax 215-7970.

Diplomatic: 122 Pau Claris, Tel. 488-0200, fax 488-1222. Located in the commercial center of the city.

Meliá Barcelona: 50 Av. Sarrià, Tel. 410-6060, 410-6173, fax 321-5179. Hotel of the highest quality; located in the commercial center of the city.

Presidente: 570 Av. Diagonal, Tel. 200-2111, fax 209-5106. This hotel is suitable for business people and is located in the new center of the city.

Barcelona Hilton: 589-591 Av. Diagonal, Tel. 419-2233, fax 405-2573. Located in the commercial center of the city.

Ritz: 668 Gran Vía de les Corts Catalanes, Tel. 318-5200, fax 318-0148. A wonderful, highly graded hoTel. One of the best hotels on the continent. It has 161 rooms, with all the necessary amenities in a lovely building in the center of the city. Starting from $300 for a single person and from $400 for a couple per night in a double room.

Almirante: 42 Vía Laietana, Tel. 268-3020, fax 268-3192. Situated in the historical center of the city, with a complete range of services; within easy access to all areas of the city.

City Park: 47 Nicaragua, Tel. 419-9500, fax 419-7163. Excellent location near the Olympic area, combines top design with practical and useful services.

EXPENSIVE HOTELS

Alexandra: 251 Mallorca, Tel. 487-0505, fax 216-0606. A good hotel in a good location.
Gran Hotel Calderón: 26 Rambla de Catalunya, Tel. 301-0000. fax 317-3157.

Colón: 7 Av. de la Catedral, Tel. 301-1404, fax 317-2915. Old hotel, near the cathedral. Excellent location.

Cóndor: 127 Vía Augusta, Tel. 209-4511, fax 202-2713. Modern hotel with standard furnishings. Located in the commercial center of the city.

Dante: 181 Mallorca, Tel. 323-2254, fax 323-7472. The hotel is located in the center of the Gothic Quarter.

Máster: 105 Valencia, Tel. 323-6215, fax 323-4389. The hotel is located in a

central area of the city, near the galleries.

Regente: 76 Rambla de Catalunya, Tel. 487-5989, fax 487-3227. The exterior renovation of the hotel looks nice, but the rooms are not particularly attractive. Avoid rooms facing the street because of the noise.

Regina Hotel: 2 Bergara, Tel. 301-3232, fax 318-2326. This hotel is located next to the Plaça de Catalunya.

Rivoli Ramblas: 128 Rambla del Estudis, Tel. 302-6643, fax 317-5053. A modern hotel (opened near the end of 1989) at the heart of the Rambla in the center of the city. The hotel is located in a handsome building, renovated in Art Deco style, with a modern lobby and comfortable rooms.

Pintor Hostel – in the Gothic Quarter

At the top of the list of this category of hotels.

Expo: 1 Mallorca, Tel. 325-1212, fax 325-1144. American style breakfast very comfortable.

Hotel Majestic: 70 Ps. de Gràcia, Tel. 488-1717, fax 488-1880. Old hotel and fascinating for those who are nostalgic for the past. Centrally located, with large, pleasant rooms, although those facing front share the noise of the busy street. Among its amenities is a swimming pool for the guests.

Royal: 117 Rambla, Tel. 301-9400, fax 317-3179. Located opposite Hotel Rivoli, but older and less expensive. Despite the unimpressive exterior and lobby, the rooms are comfortable, and the service is courteous. Excellent location.

Montecarlo: 124 Rambla del Estudis, Tel. 317-5800, fax 317-5750. After undergoing renovation, the building is handsome and impressive from the outside, but the rooms leave much to be desired. For those who suffer from noise, it is recommended not to take a front room facing the street.

TOURIST HOTELS
Ronda: 19 San Erasmo, Tel. 329-0004, fax 441-8990. The hotel is located next to the Gothic Quarter.

Rialto: 40-42 ferrán, Tel. 318-5212, fax 315-3819. Located in the heart of the city, next to the Rambla.

Belagua: 89 Vía Augusta, Tel. 237-3949, fax 415-3062. This modern up-to-date hotel is located in the commercial center of the city.

Numancia Hotel: 74 Numancia, Tel. 322-4451, fax 410-7642. A modern hotel located near the Sants train station.

Suizo Hotel: 12 Plaça del Angel, Tel. 315-4111, fax 315-3819. This old hotel has recently been renovated. It is located in the middle of the Gothic Quarter. Recommended but preferable to take one of the back rooms.

MODERATE HOTELS
Gaudí: 12 Nou de la Rambla, Tel. 317-9032, fax 412-2636. Delightful hotel, located in a quiet lane off the Rambla. The lobby is very crowded, but the service is most courteous.

Lleo: 24 Pelayo, Tel. 318-1312, fax 412-2657. Centrally located.

Oriente: 45-47 Rambla, Tel. 302-2558, fax 412-3819. The decorative lobby in this old building is handsome and pleasant for sitting in. The rooms are comfortable, and service is excellent. The reception office is very crowded, so you will have to be patient when registering or checking out.

Residencia: 47 P. Bonanova, Tel. 211-5022, fax 318-2172. Quiet, small, comfortable hotel, one of the cheapest in this category. Its greatest drawback is its relative distance from the center of the city.

Cataluña: 22 Santa Ana, Tel. 301-9150, fax 302-7870. Excellent location, in a pleasant lane off of the Rambla. The rooms are quite small, and the furnishings are not in the best taste, but the beds are very comfortable.

INEXPENSIVE HOTELS

Nouvel: 18-20 Santa Anna, Tel. 301-8274, fax 301-8370. This pleasant hotel is located in a beautiful building – although its façade could use some cleaning and repair. The high ceilings in the rooms and the decorative floors compensate for its lack of luxuries.

Lloret: 125 Ramblas de Canaletes, Tel. 317-3366, fax 301-9283. Modest hotel, without luxuries, but centrally located beside Plaça de Catalunya. The owners and staff are most pleasant. Reductions are given to those staying for a week or longer. The rooms fronting on the street are noisy.

Internacional: 78-80 Ramblas, Tel. 302-2566, fax 317-6190. An ancient and beautiful white building with pleasant rooms. The noise from the street continues until the late hours of the night and will bother those looking for a quiet and restful vacation.

Rey Don Jaime I: 11 Jaime I,

Tel. 315-4161. Charming hotel near the Gothic Quarter of the city. Quiet and safe. Suitable for young travellers.

Cortes: 25 Santa Anna, Tel. 317-9212, fax 302-7870. Centrally located.

Meson Castilla: 5 Valldoncella, Tel. 318-2182, fax 412-4020. Centrally located.

PENSIONS AND YOUTH HOSTELS

Hostal Nova: 133 Rambla de Canaletes, Tel. 412-1097. Family hotel, suitable for young travellers. Single rooms start from $12 (without windows) and double rooms from $20. The hotel is located on the third floor, and there is no elevator. The pension located above it (Hostal Canaletes) is not recommended unless you have absolutely no choice.

Kabul: 17 Pl. Reial, Tel. 318-5190. Usually occupied by young travellers. There are rooms of various sizes, which accommodate anywhere from 2 to 24 beds in a room. The hotel is located in an attractive square, but the area is not safe for single women at night. There are drug dealers and prostitutes near the hotel, but the hotel itself is safe. The atmosphere is friendly, but noisy.

Albergue Verge de Montserrat: 41-51 Marc de Déu del Coll, Tel. 210-5151. The hostel is far from the center of the city, so it is quiet, and it is almost always possible to find a vacancy there. It is located in a nice building with an impressive view. It is on the far side of Parc Güell, and can be reached via bus no. 25, 28 from the Plaça de Catalunya station. Present your youth hostel membership card.

MORE HOSTELS

Albergue Pere Tarrés: 149 Numància, Tel. 410-2309.
Hostal de Joves: 29 Passeig de Pujades, Tel. 300-3104.
Aneto: 38 C. del Carme, Tel. 318-4083.

GUESTHOUSES

Lucena: 73 C. Camélies, Tel. 284-1097.
Vicenta: 84 Rambla de Catalunya, Tel. 487-5200.

B&B

Accomodation in private homes is available through the service of Amics per sempre. Considerable discounts for longer stays (more than two weeks). For detailed pamphlet and registration form, write to *Amics per sempre*, C/València 304, 08009, Barcelona. Tel. 488-2424, fax 488-3232.

CAMPING

There are many campsites in Catalonia. The nearest to Barcelona is *Camping Barcino*, located at 50 Laurea Miró (Tel. 372-8501), only 2 kms from the city. This campsite has only 150 places, so you need to reserve a place in advance.

Larger campsites are *Cala Gogó* (9 kms south of the city, Tel. 379-4600, fax 405-2964) with 1,500 places and *El Toro Bravo* (11 kms south of the city, Tel. 637-3467) with over 2,000 places. All along road no. C-245, which goes to Sitges and to the northwest part of the country, you will find many campsites, such as *Albatros* (Tel. 662-2031) and *Tres Estrellas* (Tel. 662-1116).

Most of the campsites provide supermarkets and restaurants for their guests, and some even offer swimming pools and tennis courts. Such a campsite is the excellent *Cala Gogó*. Prices here depend on the number of vacationers. You can get more information from the camping association of Barcelona at 608 Gran Vía, Tel. 412-5955, fax 302-1336.

The language

Two official languages exist in Catalonia – Spanish, Spain's official language, and Catalan, the language of this district alone. Catalan is the language of study in the schools and is used in the local legal system and government administration. Subway and bus station signs, as well as street names, are usually written in two languages – Catalan and Castillian (Castellano, which is Spanish).

Catalan originates from the Romanesque languages; it is not a dialect of Spanish. Catalan is closer to the French spoken in southern France, than to Spanish.

```
ca – ka
co – ko
cu – ku
ce – the (voiceless)
ci – thi (voiceless)
ch – ch
ga – ha (gutteral)
go – ho (gutteral)
gu – hu (gutteral)
ge – he (gutteral)
gi – hi (gutteral)
gue – ge (hard g)
gui – gi (hard g)
ll – y
ñ – ny
j – h (gutteral)
```

All the locals speak Spanish, but at home and in the street they prefer to speak Catalan, both as a matter of pride in the district where they live and in their language, but also as part of their search for national self-identity. The publication of the first edition of a Catalan encyclopedia, was an important national event for the people of Catalonia.

To emphasize the importance of Catalan for the local people, it should be noted that in the 1992 Olympic Games both languages were used to describe various sports events.

The French language is spoken widely among Barcelonians. Young people, here as elsewhere, also know English, especially since it is the language of Pop records and Hollywood movies.

Pronunciation of the alphabet in both Castilian and Catalan differs from the way these letters are pronounced in other European languages.

Here are some rules of pronunciation in these languages:

In Catalan, vòwels at the end of the word disappear, the x is pronounced ch.

Following are a number of important words which will help you find your way around the city, written as you will find them in the tourist guides of Barcelona.

Avinguda (Av.) – avenue
Plaça (Pl.) – square
Passeig (P.) – boulevard
Ronda (Rda.) – square
Carretera (Ctra.) – road
Passatge (Ptge.) – passageway

Tourist Services

There are several permanent tourist information offices in Barcelona:

Sants Estació, Pl. Paisos Catalans. Open Mon.-Fri. 8am-8pm, Sat., Sun. and holidays 8am-2pm. Closed the first week of January and Christmas. Tel. 490-9174.

Estació França, Av. Marquès de l'Argentera. Open 8am-8pm.

Palacio de Congresos, Av.

Maria Cristina. Open daily 10am-7pm.

The International Airport Tourist Information Office, at the International Terminal: Open 9:30am-8:30pm weekdays, 9:30am-3pm weekends and holidays. Tel. 478-4704.

Patronat de Turisme de Barcelona (the Barcelona Tourist Board), and the *Barcelona Convention Bureau*, are located on 35 Passeig de Gràcia, Tel. 215-4477 fax 487-6944.

Oficina de Información Turística: 658 Gran Vía Corts Catalanes, Tel. 301-7443, fax 412-2570. Open Mon.-Fri. 9am-7pm, Sat. 9am-2pm.

Department of Tourism and Commerce, 105 Pass. de Gràcia. Tel. 237-9045, fax 238-3170.

Tourism Promotion Consortium, 112 Pass. de Gràcia. Tel. 415-1617, fax 415-1434.

There are also seasonal offices:

Ayuntamiento de Barcelona, Pl. de Sant Jaume. Open Jan. 24-Sep. 30.

Casacas Rojas (look for the red and white "I" in the Barrio Gótico and the Rambla). Open June 15- Sep. 26, 9am-9pm.

General Information

Currency and exchange

The Spanish peseta is still considered an unstable currency, even though the Spanish economy has strengthened considerably. Current exchange rates which vary slightly from day to day can be checked in the banks and newspapers. Coins are in use with values of 1, 5, 10, 25, 50, 100, 200, and 500 pesetas. Paper money is in use with values of 500, 1,000, 2,000, and 5,000 pesetas.

Money can be changed quickly and efficiently at banks. You can also change money at the large travel agencies around the Plaça da Catalunya. You pay a service charge for each type of currency you exchange, so it is not worthwhile changing small amounts of different currencies. Automatic dispensers have been set up at central places in the city (the airport, Rambla, etc.) and operate when the banks are closed. These machines, apparently, have not won the trust of either the public or the tourists.

The credit cards accepted in the large hotels and the large restaurants in Barcelona are *Visa*, *American Express*, and *Diners' Club*. Travellers' checks can also be exchanged at any bank.

Working hours

Banks: Mon.-Fri. 8:30am-2pm; Sat. 8:30am-1pm (in summer until 12:30pm). The central branches around the Plaça de Catalunya are usually open until 16:45. On Sunday, they are closed, except at the airport and train stations.

Government offices: Open Mon.-Fri. 8am-2pm and 3:30-5pm. It is always best to come before the lunch break at 2pm, because, somehow, after the siesta it is much harder to conclude your business and you may have to return the next day to wind up your affairs.

Shops: Most shops are open Mon.-Sat. 9am-1pm and 4:30-8pm. A number of large department stores, such as *El Corte Inglés* in the Plaça de Catalunya, are open straight through from 10am-8pm on Mon.-Sat. Closed on Sunday.

Restaurants are usually open for lunch from 12pm to 4:30pm and reopen for supper from 7:30-12pm.

Post offices: Most branches are open Mon.-Fri. from 9am-2pm. The central branch in Plaça Antonio Lopez is open Mon.-Fri. all day from 9am-9pm and on Sat. 9am-2pm. Closed on Sunday.

Keeping in touch

Telephones – Telephone booths are scattered all over the city. The phones work with coins of 5, 25, and 100 pesetas. In some of the booths, you can also use credit cards. You can not make collect calls from these booths, only from private telephones or from the centrally located booths at 4 Fontanelia Street.

The dialing code for Barcelona is 3 from inside Spain. If you phone Barcelona from outside Spain, the code is 343.

If you want to make an international phone call from Barcelona using direct dialing, dial 07 and then the code of the country you want. For assistance from the international operator, dial 008 (for Europe) or 005 (for the rest of the world). For additional information, dial the information service at 003.

Telegrams can be sent 24 hours a day by phoning 322-2000 or from the main post office in Plaça Antonio Lopez on weekdays between

8am-12pm and on weekends and holidays from 8am-10pm.

Stamps are sold in all tobacconist stores.

Newspapers in English, French, German and Italian can be found at the large kiosks on the Rambla. These papers are usually no more than one or two days old.

If you want to receive mail in Barcelona, ask to have it sent to the *Post Restante* in the central post office at Plaça d'Antonio Lopez – Barcelona 08000, Spain or to the American Express office at 101 Passeig de Gràcia, Tel. 217-0070 (if you have credit cards or travellers' checks from this company).

Tipping

In a restaurant it is customary to leave waiters a 10% tip. In the hotel, the elevator boy who brings you your luggage should be given about 1 dollar. The higher the rating of the hotel, the larger the tip given to its staff for the services rendered – add about 1 dollar more for each star. Taxi drivers do not take tips.

Measurements; time; electricity

The time in Barcelona is one hour later than Greenwich time. At 12 noon in Barcelona, it will be 11am in London, 12 noon in Rome and Paris, 6am in New York, and 3am in Los Angeles.

The electricity used in the city is 220-230 volts AC. Several luxury hotels use 110-120 volts current for safety reasons.

The metric system of measurement is used in Barcelona: weights are given in kilograms; clothing and shoe sizes are the same as those in use throughout Europe.

BARCELONA

GETTING TO KNOW THE CITY

It is easy to get around Barcelona because the city is concentrated in a relatively small area, between the hills and the port. The city center is a large square, Plaça de Catalunya. A wide thoroughfare, Rambla Boulevard, which is the main artery of the city, leads south from the square, connecting it to the port (Puerto y Barcelona). East of the boulevard is the famous old quarter, the Gothic Quarter (Barrio Gótico), and, at its center, is the cathedral (Catedral), the hub of Barcelona tourism. Vía Laietana separates the Gothic Quarter from the Ribera Quarter (Barrio Ribera), where there are also many tourist sites, such as the Picasso Museum.

Interesting architecture and patches of green – a view of Barcelona from the Columbus Monument

The Passeig de Gràcia leads north from the Plaça de Catalunya, toward the hills. This street is the commercial heart of the city: the large banks and many airlines have their offices here. It traverses the modern and busy Eixample Quarter, which is a center for activities not related to tourism – though the best works of Gaudí, such as the Sacred Family Church (Sagrada Familia) are found here.

Montjuïc Hill is adjacent to the sea, on the southwest, and has many tourist attractions, such as the Spanish village (Poble Espanyol). Tibidabo Hill, north of the city, offers several marvelous lookout points. These two hills serve as clear landmarks, and help you find your bearings in the city.

Organized tours

Julia Tours (Tel. 317-6454 or 317-6209) and *Pullmantour* (635 José-Antonio Street, not far from Plaça de Catalunya, Tel. 317-1297) are two agencies specializing in guided tours (in Spanish, French, English and Italian). They offer morning tours (9:30am-12:30pm); afternoon tours (3:30-6:30pm); day tours (9:30am-6:30pm); night and flamenco tours (Thurs., Sat., starting at 9:15pm) and many other attractions.

Tour boats afloat at the port

The *Bus Turistic* line is a 15 stop circuit of the major Barcelona sites. It operates between June 1-October 12 and is wonderful for an overall view of the city's highlights. The first bus leaves Plaça de Catalunya at 9:30am, the last at 7:30pm. Buses run every twenty minutes. The Bus Turistic ticket offers various reductions and discounts on entrance fees to tourist sites. You can get on or off the bus at any of the stations and continue your tour of the city on a later bus.

The *Las Golondrinas* company operates boat trips along the docks to the lighthouse at the end of the harbor. The boats depart from the Portal de la Pau, and the trip takes about half an hour.

BARCELONA

1. Plaça de Catalunya
2. The Ramblas
3. The Gothic Quarter
4. Columbus Monument
5. The port
6. Montjuïc and the Olympic Center
7. Poble Espanyol
8. Plaça d'Espanya
9. Joan Miró Park
10. Sants-Central railway station
11. The Citadel Park
12. La Barceloneta
13. Post Office
14. Plaça de Toros Monumental
15. Sagrada Familia
16. Güell Park
17. Tibidabo
18. F.C. Barcelona Stadium
19. Eixample
20. Pedralbes Palace
21. Pedralbes Monastery

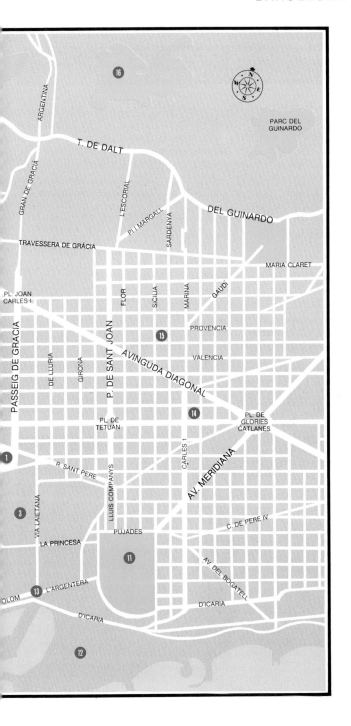

PARC DEL
GUINARDO

ARGENTINA

T. DE DALT

GRAN DE GRÁCIA

L'ESCORIAL

P. I MARGALL

SARDENYA

DEL GUINARDO

TRAVESSERA DE GRÁCIA

MARIA CLARET

PL. JOAN
CARLES I

FLOR

SICILIA

MARINA

GAUDÍ

PASSEIG DE GRACIA

DE LLÚRIA

GIRONA

P. DE SANT JOAN

PROVENCIA

⑮

AVINGUDA DIAGONAL

VALENCIA

PL. DE
TETUAN

⑭

PL. DE
GLORIES
CATLANES

❶

R. SANT PERE

LLUIS COMPANYS

CARLES 1

AV. MERIDIANA

❸

VIA LAIETANA

C. DE PERE IV

PUJADES

LA PRINCESA

AV. DEL BOGATELL

⑪

OLOM

⑬ L'ARGENTERA

D'ICARIA

D'ICARIA

⑫

The Gothic Quarter – The Ancient Heart of the City

Since Roman times, through the Middle Ages, this quarter has been the very heart of Barcelona. In the past it was called **Barrio Romano**, a reminder of the Roman period which left its mark. Now, everyone calls it **Barrio Gótico**, the Gothic Quarter, after the style of building commonly used in Barcelona between the twelfth and fifteenth centuries. Today, the quarter is encircled by the streets which connect four squares and form almost a perfect quadrangle. The squares are:

On the north – Plaça Antoni Maura
On the west – Plaça Nova
On the south – Plaça de Sant Jaume
On the east – Plaça Emili Vilanova

Bus lines which operate to the east of the Gothic Quarter are nos. 16, 17, and 45 on Vía Laietana. The first (and last) station of line 19 is in Avinguda Catedral, north of the quarter. The nearest subway station, in the southeast corner of the quarter, is Jaume I of line L4 (the yellow line).

A water fountain and spindley trees give an enchanting touch to Plaça Sant Felip Neri

Despite the many improvements, repairs, renovations and changes which the quarter has undergone during the previous centuries, it still retains the special charm of a medieval city: the narrow lanes, the juxtaposition of the buildings, verandas which almost touch each other, with only a narrow strip of sky visible between the buildings. In most of its old streets, families still live in the old houses, children run about below, shops continue to sell their wares and the enticing smell of the dishes being prepared in the restaurant kitchens wafts through the air. All these bring this ancient quarter to life and make wandering through it a rich experience. We begin our tour in the western corner of the quarter, at **Plaça Nova**, a thirteenth century market place. There is probably no spot more appropriate for entering the quarter than between the two impressive round towers of the **Bishop's Gate** (Portal del Bisbe). This gate is a remnant of a first century AD Roman wall which collapsed when it could not withstand the barbarian attacks. The towers were erected in the Middle Ages, as part of the building to their right, the **Bishop's Palace** (Palau Episcopal). Construction of this building began at the end of the twelfth century and was completed at the beginning of the thirteenth. Its foundations embrace the remains of the Roman wall. The façade of the building, stark and grey, was rebuilt in the second half of the eighteenth century. If the gate is open, you can go in and look at the courtyard, surrounded by arches in the Roman style.

A courtyard which should not be missed awaits you in the building to the left, the

Flowers spilling over the delicately structured courtyard of the house of the Archdeacon

House of the Archdeacon (Casa de l'Ardiaca). It was built in the sixteenth century (on the remains of an earlier structure from the eleventh century) for the Archdeacon Don Despla in mixed Gothic and Renaissance style. Since 1919, it serves as the home of the Institute of Municipal History.

Turning left to Carrer de Santa Llucia, on your left you will see the gate of a building.

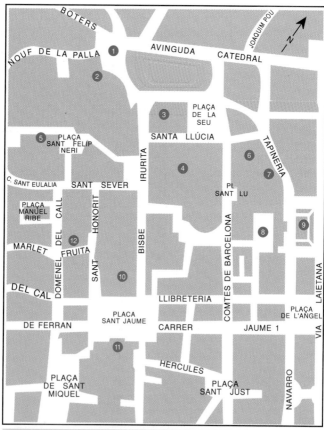

THE GOTHIC QUARTER

1. Plaça Nova
2. The Bishop's Palace
3. House of the Archdeacon
4. The Cathedral
5. Museum of Old Shoes
6. Frederic Marés museum
7. Royal Palace
8. Plaça del Rei
9. Plaça Ramón Berenguer el Gran
10. Catalonian Government Palace
11. City Hall
12. The Jewish Quarter

On entering, you will immediately feel the magic of this charming place: a small marvellous world consisting entirely of a square yard, enclosed by a veranda on pillars. At its center is a water fountain which flows into a small pool. In the pool, if they have not yet wilted, water lilies are growing. To the right of the pool rises a thin-stemmed palm tree, which is as tall as the building. Because of its age, it is supported by ropes attached to its trunk. All around, on the walls of the courtyard, is a series of ceramic tiles, painted in cheerful hues of blue, green, and yellow, depicting flowering potted plants interspersed with fish, birds, and snails. You can sit on the cool stone bench next to the wall (to the left of the entrance) and enjoy the scenery.

Plaça de la Seu – the impressive Gothic façade of the Cathedral

From the courtyard, a stairway leads to the pillared veranda. From up here, there is a better view of the building's windows, each of which is decorated with different forms of carved stone. You can also glance at the wall of the neighboring cathedral, where statues of winged animals are hanging. To the left, as we leave the House of the Archdeacon, the street leads to the broad **Plaça de la Seu**, where we find the main entrance to the **Cathedral** (Catedral) of Barcelona. Open daily 8am-1:30pm and 4-7:30pm. Tel. 315-1554.

Construction of the cathedral began in the last years of the thirteenth century, and it took more than 150 years until its dedication

Worshipping in red candle-light at the Barcelona Cathedral

in 1450. The façade and the pointed towers we see today are relatively new. They were erected at the end of the nineteenth century, instead of the towers that were there in the first place, which had not withstood the ravages of time. The construction took place according to the original plans of the cathedral, preserving its Gothic-Catalonian style. The interior of the cathedral is majestic: high pillars support the ceiling, light spills in through the stained glass of the elongated windows and through the small circular windows near the ceiling.

All around are chapels of influential families, with treasures of religious art – various paintings, sculptures, and hand wrought metal objects. The apse, enclosed on three sides, is surrounded by marvelously delicate carvings, the work of the fifteenth century German sculptor Lochner.

We step out into the cathedral courtyard, where there is a very different atmosphere, much less severe. In the center of the yard, surrounded by stone arches on all sides, we find palm trees, tall loquats, and magnolias. In one of the corners of the garden, beside a pool of water, there is a flock of red-billed geese investigating the goings on.

Between the chapels which surround the garden you will find the entrance to the **Cathedral Museum** (Museu de la Catedral), Tel. 315-1554. It is open every day from 11am-1pm (entrance fee). This is a very small museum, but worth visiting, if only to see at least one of the masterpieces, located to the right of the entrance of the second room. It is *La Pietat*, the work of Bartolome Bermejo, painted in 1490.

Leaving the inner garden of the cathedral brings us to a rectangular area. On the right, a winding street, Carrer Montjuïc del Bisbe, turns to the west. At the end of the street, we find ourselves in a pleasant square, **Plaça Sant Felip Neri**. It is one of the more poetic spots in the quarter. There is a fountain in the center of the square, where flocks of doves gather to drink, with two imposing trees on either side – the simplicity is captivating.

Upon entering the square, on the left is the entrance to a small but very entertaining museum. It is the **Museum of Old Shoes** (Museu del Calçat Antic). Open Tues.-Sun. 11am-2pm and 5-8pm, closed Mondays (entrance fee). Tel. 301-4533.

Usually there are not many visitors here. The guard at the entrance puts on the lights in the exhibition hall, when a visitor arrives. In this not very large room are glass exhibition cases containing the finest footwear of past generations. Pointed women's shoes, made of velvet and silk, from the seventeenth, eighteenth, and nineteenth centuries; the shoes of noblemen who roamed through the Spanish palaces, gigantic leather boots of some person of stature from the fourteenth century, sandals of priests from the thirteenth century, shoes of wood, straw, rope, goat skin, and more. For a special treat, several pairs of shoes of famous people are

One could walk for miles in yesterday's styles – a display at the Museum of Old Shoes

exhibited, the most famous belonging to Pablo Casals.

Returning to the square brings us to Carrer del Bisbe, where we turn right. From this street we take the first turn left to Carrer de la Pietat, which meanders to the right to Carrer del Paradis, all in order to get to house no. 10 on this street. Officially, the place is open to visitors Fri.-Mon. from 6-9:30pm, but it is possible to enter at other times by simply pushing the heavy wooden door which opens onto the street. This is the **Center for the Study of Catalonia** (Centre Excursionista de Catalunya).

In the dark entrance hallway, in the far right corner, is the most important Roman relic in Barcelona – four of the pillars from the Roman temple, erected in honor of Augustus. These impressive pillars, along with a hypothetical sketch of the temple, help us recapture the times when such a splendid structure was located here.

The impressive Royal Palace

We return to the street (Paradis), going right to Baixada Santa Clara. We are now behind the cathedral – giving us another opportunity to look at it. From here, a left turn on Carrer dels Contes will bring us to a palace which was formerly the home of the king's courtiers and, today, is the **Archive of the Crown of Aragón** (Arxiu – de la Corona d'Arago). The palace was built in the sixteenth century in late Gothic style, with Renaissance motifs, under the direction of the architect Antoni Carbonell.

Further along, the street widens and becomes a small, rectangular square, Plaça Sant lu. Here, we have the entrance to the **Frederic Marés Museum** (Museu Frederic Marés), Metro L4,

Jaume I, located in part of what used to be the palace of Barcelona nobility and, later, of the kings of Aragón and Catalonia. The museum is open Tues.-Sat. 10am-5pm, Sun. and holidays 10am-2pm. Closed on Monday. Tel. 310-5800. There is a weekday entrance fee; free admission on Sundays.

The collections in this museum were donated to the city of Barcelona by the sculptor Frederic Marés, who lived at the end of the nineteenth and the beginning of the twentieth century. The museum affords sculpture enthusiasts a good opportunity to enjoy a range of works from the eleventh through the eighteenth centuries, including wooden statues of Jesus on the cross and of the saints, which were previously housed in different churches throughout the country. On the first floor of the museum, you can view burial rooms, from the sixteenth century. On the second and third storeys of the museum you will find on exhibit a rich collection of objects from daily life which were in use during various periods.

Meandering down the Gothic lanes in the wintry sun

Outside the museum, in Sant Lu Square, a stairway leads up to the **Royal Palace** (Palau Reial Major) and in to an impressive hall, Saló del Tinell. Here, in the fourteenth century, stood the throne. It is said that it was here that the "Catholic monarchs" Ferdinand and Isabella received Christopher Columbus, when he returned from his first journey to America. Mighty stone arches support the ceiling of the hall, which still gives the impression of power and majesty.

We return to Contes Street and turn left to Baixada Santa Clara, and left again. On the way, we can look right, toward a narrow lane, whose entrance is blocked by a metal gate – an excellent example of all that has been said about the narrow streets so typical of a medieval city. Only a short distance further on, we find the **Plaça del Rei** in all

Clariana-Padellas House, which houses the City History Museum

its glory. It is surrounded by buildings – the king's palace and the windows of the throne room face it. Overlooking the scene is a tall observation tower, five storeys high, with seven large windows on each floor, which enabled the guards to see over a great distance. The tower, named after King Martin (Torre del Rei Martí), is mistakenly associated with him; it was only added to the palace in the sixteenth century. At the opposite end of the square is another tower, over the **Capella de Santa Agata**, which was built as a house of worship for members of the royal family in the thirteenth century. Next to it, on the southeastern side of the square, is another Gothic structure called Clariana-Padellas House, which houses the **City History Museum** (Museu d'Historia de la Ciutat). Open Tues.-Fri. 10am-2pm and 4-8pm, Sat. 10am-2pm, closed Sun., Mon. and holidays. The entrance to the museum is from Carrer Veguer. It is open Tues.-Sun. from 9am-2pm, 3:30-8:30pm; closed Mondays and also Sunday afternoons. Tel. 315-1111. There is an entrance fee; free admission on Sundays.

The low basement floor of this museum is so "deep" that it reaches the Roman foundations of Barcelona, which, in itself, is sufficient justification for a visit to the site. The dim light here imparts a magic aura to the old stones and confers a special feeling of a visit to a place where time has stood still. The remains of houses, the paths between them, the water cistern, the ceramic pipes indicating the high level of urban sanitation, various inscriptions on the stones – all bear witness to the life of the citizens of Barcino in the fourth century.

The remains of the handsome mosaics include one especially beautiful specimen which has been reconstructed. It depicts three women in purple, standing naked, next to each other. We can learn about the daily life from the remains of household items: millstones, well-made stone mortar and pestles, huge wheat urns, slender jugs of wine and oil, etc. Some of these relics have been left half embedded in the earth, just as they were found by the archaeologists.

In the entrance floor of the museum, to the right of the ticket counter, a side door leads to a small wing. Here, you will find the remains of the Jewish cemetery which were uncovered during the Montjuïc excavations in 1945, with graves dating from the eleventh to the fourteenth centuries.

A Roman inscription at the City History Museum

On the way up to the next floor, on the staircase, is a fine exhibit of copper containers, which were used to measure liquids in the sixteenth to the nineteenth centuries. In the various halls on this floor are items of furniture, paintings, embroidery, everyday objects, and miniatures which tell the history of the city during different periods. In a side room you will find the "Grand Clock" (El Gran Rellotge), which was built in 1576 and served as the public clock of Barcelona for 217 years. It was restored in 1976 and placed on exhibit in the museum.

In another room (off hall XV), is an exhibition of artistically illuminated books from the seventeenth and eighteenth centuries.

On leaving the museum, we go left, around the group of buildings, to reach the rear of the king's palace. Here is the square named after the count of Barcelona, **Plaça Ramón Berenguer el Gran**. There is a small garden, with benches, a place to relax for a moment and to look at the wall of the palace, which "incorporates" the ancient

The Catalonian Government Palace – a building of contrasting styles.

Roman wall in its lower part, and seems to be an extension of it. In the center of the square is a bronze statue of Ramón Berenguer.

Heading back to the right, to Vía Llibreteria Street, we reach a wide square, **Plaça de Sant Jaume**. This is the juncture of the two main Roman roads of the old city, the Cardus and the De-cumanus. This was the heart of the public area, the scene of public assemblies, official celebrations and ceremonies, the location of the forum and the market. Today, there are two very impressive structures here: the **Catalonian Government Palace** (Palau de la Generalitat) and the **Barcelona City Hall** (Casa de la Ciutat).

Unarranged visits to the Government Palace are not possible. Organized tours for groups take place only on Sundays between 10am-1pm, but it is necessary to register in advance, in writing to: Palau de la Generalitat, Barcelona, Protocolo, Olga Castells.

You can also try your luck and come when a tour is scheduled to take place and join it. If you succeed, it will be well worth your while. The government palace is an historical symbol rich in memories and of considerable importance for Catalonians. Today, along with government offices, it houses the office of the President of Catalonia. The overhead passage in neo-Gothic style (erected in this century), seen from Carrer del Bisbe, leads to the President's official residence.

This large structure consists of various wings, built in different periods. Its interior was formed by joining two houses, acquired in 1403, which were renovated, furnished, and decorated by the architect Marc Safont, in order to serve as the seat of government (*Generalitat*). During the course of the fifteenth and sixteenth centuries, several wings and halls were added with the

Ramón Berenguer, the count of Barcelona.

work of four different architects. At the beginning of the seventeenth century, the front façade (facing the square) was built in Renaissance style, and the rear façade in baroque style, by the architect Pere Pau Ferrer.

A walk around the palace reveals several works which deserve our attention. At the frontage, over the entrance gate, inside a rounded niche, is the statue of St. George (Sant Jordi), mounted on a horse, battling the dragon. This marble statue from 1860 is the work of Andreu Aleu, honoring the patron saint of the government of Catalonia. In the street to the right of the front façade (del Bisbe) is the gateway to the medieval wing of the palace, which was built in 1418 by Marc Safont, with a sculpted coping in the Gothic style typical of that period. Next to it is the overhead passage which we have already mentioned.

The Catalonian Government Palace has undergone many additions throughout the years

On our tour of the palace grounds, there are a number of stopping points where you

can see objects of beauty and grandeur. The best-known and most popular spot is the **Orange Tree Courtyard** (Pati dels Tarongers). The Catalonians flock here when there is "Open House" at the palace on April 23, St. George's Day. In the courtyard, orange trees have been planted – dwarf trees, which, when in flower, give off an intoxicating fragrance. Amidst them is a water fountain, and on top of it, a miniature statue of St. George, by the sculptor Frederic Galcera, completed in 1926.

The middle level of the inner courtyard of the palace is surrounded with rows of arches supported by slender stone pillars, which recall the inner courts of the Catalonian monasteries. A decorative staircase, built in 1425, leads to one of the corners of the courtyard.

In the Old City

Opposite is the main entrance to the chapel of St. George, which is a work of art in stone carving. The delicacy of the cherubs is evocative of lacework. The square inner room of the chapel is decorated with wall hangings from Venice and Florence, and has valuable old sacred objects on display. Here, in the presence of the President and the Catalonian notables, the Archbishop of Barcelona recites the festive mass on St. George's Day.

The Room of St. George (Salon de Sant-Jordi), the most luxurious room in the palace, looks down from the first floor on Plaça Sant Jaume. The room's ceiling is the suspension dome of the palace, which is decorated on the inside with impressive wall paintings, depicting historical and allegorical events. Some of the wall paintings are from the sixteenth century, and others were restored after having been damaged during

the Civil War. Originally, it was planned to bring the palace chapel to this room, but eventually, the dome was built, and it became the venue for grand receptions and important ceremonies. These all take place by the light of the large crystal chandelier, which weighs about two tons.

The gates of the palace are open to all on the day of celebration (April 23). On that day the inner court is decorated with thousands of red roses. The stalls in the square sell books. Roses and books – the symbols of love and culture.

Opposite the government palace is the **City Hall of Barcelona** (Casa de la Ciutat, or the Ajuntament). It is open to visitors every day from 10am-1pm and 4:30-7:30pm, but this is subject to change, There is an information bureau inside, to the left of the main entrance.

In the alleys of the Gothic Quarter

This large Gothic structure, built in the second half of the fourteenth century, has been "encased" almost completely by neo-classical façades (you can still see the remains of the original façade on the side facing the Carrer de la Ciutat). The "Salon of the Council of the Hundred" (Saló del Consell de Cent) is the most famous hall in the building, and it attracts many visitors. It was planned and built in 1373 by the architect Pere Llobet and is very impressive because of its massive stone walls, its large arches which support the decorated ceiling, and the ancient candelabra (originally intended to hold hundreds of candles).

West of the Government Palace, between Carrer del Call, Carrer Sant Sever, and Carrer Banys, is the **Jewish Quarter** which thrived during the eleventh to thirteenth centuries. The Jewish Quarter of

Barcelona was crowded, alive and bustling: its many intellectuals, poets, and writers, greatly influenced the life and culture of the city. The neighborhood merchants and its men of means financed many projects – including voyages of naval conquest. All this took place, until the end of the fifteenth century, when hatred of the Jews led to the destruction of the quarter and the exile of its inhabitants.

In one of the lanes of the present day quarter, Carrer de Marlet, the municipality has erected a replica of the tombstone with the Hebrew inscription, "The holy Rabbi Shmuel the Serb." The original stone is on exhibit in the City History Museum, as a reminder of what the quarter was like in earlier times.

We are back at Plaça Sant Jaume. From the southeast corner of the square, we go via Carrer de la Ciutat and immediately left on Carrer d'Hércules to a small square, Plaça Sant Just.

The Gothic **Església dels Sants Just i**

Paston, whose entrance faces the square, is known to be the oldest of Barcelona's churches. Ancient documents attest that in the tenth century it already had been accorded important status and authority throughout Spain (Valider les Testaments Sacramentels).

A small lane going east from the square is Carrer del Bisbe Cassador, which ends in front of a large building: the Royal Academy of Literature. Behind it (you can go around the group of buildings by returning to the square and turning left and left again) are more remains of the Roman wall, at the foot of **Plaça Emili Vilanova** – the square where we conclude our tour of the Gothic Quarter.

The Rambla — Barcelona's Main Artery

This is the heart of Barcelona, the colorful, popular, almost non-stop channel of its activity. It is almost two kilometers long and located on the gentle slope between Plaça de Catalunya and the port. Sometimes its name appears in its plural form, Ramblas, because the wide promenade is divided into sections with different names, all beginning La Rambla: Canaletes, Estudis, Sant Josep, Caputxins, Santa Mónica, but house numbers continue consecutively from one end to the other, as if it were one street.

It is easy to get to the starting point for our tour, at **Plaça de Catalunya**. This is an important center of the city, a juncture for transport, shopping, business, and touring. Two subway lines bring you here: L1 (red) and L3 (green), as well as trains, with a direct connection to the airport and the central railroad station (Sants). Many buses from all directions pass the various corners of the square: 16, 17, 19, 22, 24, 28, 39 and others.

On both sides of the Rambla, there are narrow sidewalks which extend the full length of the street: next to each sidewalk, is a one-way road for vehicular traffic while, in the center, is the promenade itself. Along

The beginning of the 2km action-packed Ramblas

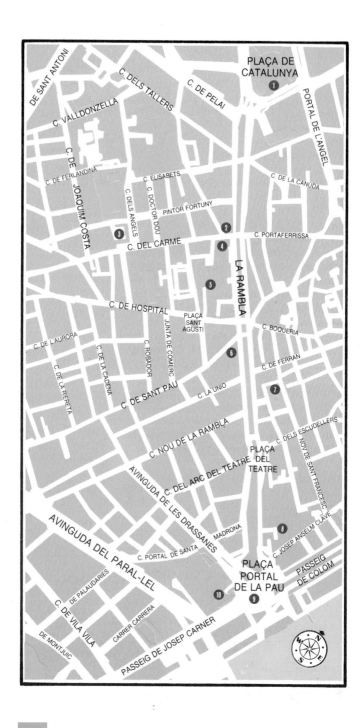

the entire stretch of the Rambla, there are large overhanging trees providing shade for pedestrians, and innumerable kiosks, which are open until late at night, selling newspapers, books and other publications. Here, tourists can find newspapers in English, French, German, and Italian. Alongside the kiosks are stalls selling flowers, potted plants, and birds. The scene is completed by the presence of vendors selling cigarettes, pictures, toys, and assorted souvenirs. In one section, fortune tellers and playing card diviners have set up their tables. During the week and especially on Sundays, musicians come to the Rambla along with clowns, acrobats, and other street artists, attracting crowds around them and performing for the price of the coins thrown into their hats.

In the many cafés which have set up tables, under the shady trees along the Rambla, you can order either a cold or hot drink, ice cream or something tasty to eat. Also, at intervals of about ten meters there are white chairs grouped together. The manager of this concession, identified by his hat, may ask for a few pesetas for the use of a chair.

The upper part of the Rambla, nearest to Plaça de Catalunya, is more elegant. Here, there are luxury hotels and prestigious shops. The lower part, nearest the harbor, is characterized by halls with sex shows and, in the afternoon and evening, "working

RAMBLA

1. Plaça de Catalunya
2. Betlem church
3. Hospital de Sant Creu
4. Palau de la Virreina
5. The covered market
6. The Opera Building
7. Plaça Reial
8. Wax Museum
9. Monument a Colom
10. Maritime Museum

girls" take to their stations to wait for customers. If this type of entertainment is not to your taste, and you walk here late at night, you should know what the hazards are. In any case, the local police are very much in evidence and, almost everywhere, at all hours, on the promenade and in the narrow lanes which branch off from it, there are patrols keeping watch.

The Rambla is also the main artery connecting interesting sites, and, in addition to simply exploring the street itself, it is certainly worth leaving the promenade to the right and left in order to see these attractions. You can quench your thirst at the handsome fountain on the wall, at building no. 116. Here, above the water taps is a painting on ceramic tiles depicting a medieval market outside the walls. At no. 118 of the same street is the bookstore of Catalonian government publications where you can find a selection of albums, guides, and posters.

The enchanting garden at St. Creu Hospital awaits you free of charge all day long

To the right, at the corner of Carrer del Carme, is the **Betlem Church** (Església de Betlem). Some may find this church impressive, but since it was badly damaged during the civil war, in 1936, and carelessly renovated, it has lost its charm. Turn right on Carrer del Carme Street until you reach number 47. This is the massive structure of the **Hospital de Santa Creu**, an old hospital, erected in the thirteenth century. In its various wings, we find the Royal Academy of Medicine and Surgery and the Institute for Catalan Studies, including a large Catalonian library.

But most interesting of all for the tourist is the garden of the hospital, to which there is free

A street corner on the Rambla

access during the day. It is worth visiting to enjoy the lovely combination of the old building, the trees, the flower beds and the pool of water in the middle.

From the garden you can go out to the street, which is parallel to the Carme on the south, called Carrer del Hospital. To the left, we find a building which served in the past as a hospital church. Today, it contains a pleasant gallery. Notice the lovely wood carvings above the entrance door.

Returning to the Rambla, we turn left to no. 99 where the impressive **Palau de la Virreina** is located. This was the palace of the wife of the Spanish viceroy in Peru, from the second half of the eighteenth century. Today, its broad confines house the offices of the culture section of the Barcelona municipality, as well as a museum of stamps and coins. The museum is open Tues.-Sun.

Colors galore, fresh fruit and vegetable stalls at the covered market

from 10am-2pm and 4:30-9:30pm; closed on Mondays and on Sunday afternoons. Tel. 301-7775. There is an entrance fee; free admission on Sundays.

You may find only temporary exhibitions in this museum, replacing the permanent ones, which for some reason may be closed to the public at the time of your visit. In the palace courtyard you may find a self-service information stand. A video monitor gives all kinds of free information about what's on in Barcelona at the push of a button.

A turn to the right after house no. 91 takes us into a completely different world. This is the **covered market** (Mercat de la Boqueria), also called the Sant Josep Market. Its metal structure was erected in the last century. Every day of the week, during the morning and after the noon siesta, its hundreds of stalls sparkle with a wealth of color, wafting the pungent smells of fruits and vegetables, fish and shellfish, cheeses, meats, and other delicacies that Catalonia has to offer. At the market, you can put together an interesting meal to enjoy while seated in one of the chairs along the promenade and, for dessert, find a pastry at the *Escriba* confectionery, a little further down at no. 83. Its cakes are as tasty as the shop is marvellously decorated shop.

The Opera Building (Gran Teatre del Liceu) used to stand at no. 63 of the Rambla. It was one of the most important opera houses in the world and the favourite of several renowned singers. The Liceu, originally designed by Oriol Mestres, opened in 1847, but was destroyed by fire some years later. It was reconstructed and reopened in 1862. The architect, Ignasi Soláj, undertook a rapid renovation of its infrastructure maintaining the original façade and features of the building. In 1994 another fire broke out and destroyed the building completely.

A right turn on Carrer Nou de la Rambla takes us to the **Güell Palace** (Palau Güell), which Gaudí built for the Güell family. The building is located at no. 3 of this street and, today, it houses the Theater Institute of Barcelona, which presents exhibitions on various topics connected with the stage and performing arts (see the chapter on "Gaudí's Barcelona").

In the other direction, to the left, take a short walk up the Carrer de Colom to one of the most impressive squares in the city: **Plaça Reial** (Royal Square), which is both broad and square and lives up to its name. Look around and feel the complete harmony of the buildings which enclose the square, all uniform in style, with white-yellow color and iron porches. The entire length of the rooftops is decorated with a balustrade of white posts. In the center of the square, is a bronze water fountain, painted black, with three lovely maidens carrying a large shell on their heads. Around the square, are scattered high palm trees and lamp posts with clusters of lights. Many pleasant cafés and restaurants are nestled among the gallery of arches around the periphery and, in one of the bays, we even find a police station (in a caravan), a reminder of the many disturbances and attacks on pedes-

The Rambla – a green artery in the center of the bustling city

trians which took place here, not so long ago, thus necessitating permanent police presence.

The best day to see the square is on Sunday: it is the day when countless vendors gather here to sell stamps, coins, gems, books, and all manner of goods. Sometimes, there is even an orchestra playing to add to your enjoyment as you browse. At night time, however, it is often deserted and may become somewhat unpleasant. Be careful!

A collection of impressive state buildings around the port's plaza

Again, back to the Rambla, until we reach the Plaça del Teatre (Theater Square). This is when the district usually changes its character and becomes slightly more menacing. The dimly lit lanes leading off to the right bring us to the **Chinese Quarter** (Barrio Chino), which has a bad reputation. If you are looking for certain kinds of bars, forbidden pleasures, and even a bit of danger, this is the place. What you won't find here is anything at all to do with the Chinese.

Something very different is located at the end of a narrow street between houses no. 4 and no. 6, to the left. It is the **Wax Museum** of Barcelona (Museu Cera), very popular with both young and old. Open daily 10am-2pm and 4-8pm; On weekends, 10am-8pm.

Tel. 317-2649. There is an entrance fee; half price for children up to age 11.

If you have seen other wax museums, then this one is nothing special – but if you have never seen a wax museum, you can certainly enjoy it. In the first room, you can see the deceased Persian Shah, King Hussein, Charles and Diana, Indira Ghandi, the Belgian king and queen, and Archbishop Makarios all "listening" to the playing of Pablo Casals and Andres Segovia. Via the corridor of children's fables, between Pinocchio, Cinderella, Red Riding Hood, and Superman, we reach the "Political Corner", where we find a roundup of famous personages placed next to each other: Lenin, Churchill, Franco, Nixon, Che Guevera, Mussolini, De Gaulle, the king and queen of Spain, Ben Gurion... and Hitler. And don't forget the "Hall of Horrors" on the basement floor.

The large, busy port of Barcelona

Returning to the Rambla, we reach the end of the promenade, opposite a large square which faces the sea and the port, **Plaça Portal de la Pau**, with a memorial monument at

its center honoring Christopher Columbus (Monument a Colom). The discoverer of the American continent is cast in bronze, placed on top of the column, with his hand pointing out to the sea. The height of the column is about 50 meters, and it was the work of Gaietá Buigas, dedicated on the occasion of the international exhibition in 1888. At its base, facing the sea, is an opening. Here, we descend in order to ascend by elevator to the observation lookout at the foot of the statue of Columbus. Open Tues.-Sat. 10am-2pm and 3:30-6pm; in summer and on Sundays, open 10am-7pm. Closed on Mondays. There is an entrance fee, 50% reduction on Sundays and holidays. From here, there is an extraordinary view, especially of the large port below.

Columbus in bronze, 50 meters high stands on his impressive monument

Around the square are large, elegant buildings, among them, the military headquarters of Catalonia, the naval command, and the customs house of the port.

West of the square you will find the **Maritime Museum** (Museu Marítimo), located in the old shipyard of Barcelona. It is open Tues.-Sat. 9:30am-1pm and 4-7pm. Closed on Mondays, Sundays and holidays. Tel. 318-3245.

There could be no more appropriate a place for this museum than the ancient building of the shipyards of Barcelona, originally erected in the thirteenth century. For hundreds of years, until the beginning of the eighteenth century, shipyard workers toiled in this building, under the vaulted stone ceilings, and sent down to the sea hundreds of merchant ships and warships. Later, the building, which was wondrously well-preserved, was used for different purposes, especially by the army. At the beginning of the 1940's, after it was given over to the municipality, it became a museum. Various historical documents, the earliest from 1243, tell of the different projects, by order of kings and generals, which were undertaken by the shipyards. It should be remembered that in those days, the sea reached the very spot where the building stands, and the boats were launched from the workrooms directly into the sea. Today, the museum has added various items from all over Spain, and elsewhere, to its local Catalonian collections, so that it is now one of the most important museums of its kind in the world.

At the Maritime Museum

In the center of the large hall, the entrance hall, is the museum's crowning glory: the royal flagship Real, which led the Spanish fleet to its great victory in the battle against the Turkish fleet in 1571. Of course, this is not the original boat, but an exact reproduction, which still makes a grand impression.

Beautiful white architecture at Barcelona's naval school

SECTOR NAVAL DE CATALUÑA

One of many exhibits at the Maritine Museum

It weighs 237 tons and is 60 meters long. On each side it has two rows of 21 giant oars, its stern is gilded, richly embossed with paintings and wood carvings and it has three large lamps hanging in the front. The prow of the boat is long and pointed, like the snout of the swordfish, and at its tip is the figure of a mythological god. By exploiting lookout points which are reached by steps, it is possible to climb to the level of the parapet and look down at the rows of seats of the oarsmen, the ship's bridge, the captain's cabin, and the royal deck cabin in the stern.

In other parts of the large hall, there are relics of ships' anchors from the Roman period and reliefs from the Arab period; models of ships from various other periods, original ancient boats, heavy cannons from the decks of warships of the Spanish Armada, and stone and metal cannonballs. And, from the nineteenth century there is furniture from passenger boats, sleeping cabins, and the cabin which served as the office of the captain of the "Galatea", which was built for the Spanish fleet in Glasgow in 1896. Nearby is a special exhibit which reviews the development of steamships and has a huge steam engine from one of the first ships of its kind, proudly on display.

From the entrance hall, we move on to a building in the rear, where, on the second floor, is another extensive display. At the entrance, is a collection of figureheads from various ships – beautiful maidens or fierce looking men, whose visage the sailors hoped would somehow calm the sea.

Inside the hall, devoted to King Pedro IV, hero of the port battle which took place in Barcelona in 1359, is a corner honoring Columbus – models of the ships with which he set out on the historical voyage of the discovery of America, his flags and various drawings.

Throughout the room are exhibited models of royal Egyptian ships which led courageous voyages up the Nile (2040-1785 BC), and numerous compasses and navigational instruments from different periods. Actually, everything that is connected with maritime history is displayed here: binoculars, fire-lamps of boats, flags, eating implements used by the sailors, and even the famous "ships in bottles".

Before leaving the room, on the right, is a side room with several ancient and rare nautical maps. The most important, the work of a fifteenth century cartographer, was in use by the explorer Amerigo Vespucci, the man after whom the American continents are named. A map of the Mediterranean Sea, drawn by Bartolomeu Olives in 1538, also catches the eye.

When we leave the Maritime Museum, nothing would be more natural than to go down to the **port**. The *Santa María*, an exact reproduction of the ship in which Columbus sailed to the new world, used to anchor near the wharf, opposite the Columbus Monument. Unfortunately, it sank after a fire.

We continue with a pleasant walk along the docks of the port, where many ships, sailboats, and yachts are anchored. Opposite, stand two high metal towers – used for the *Telefèric* cablecar which goes up to Montjuïc. This cablecar leaves from the port, and tickets for it can be purchased at Portal de la Pau. You can settle for a ride up in the elevator to observe the surroundings and especially the harbor area.

Another way to appreciate the size of the port of Barcelona would be to take a boat

ride on one of the tour boats anchored at the dock next to the Portal de la Pau Square. The company which operates these boats, *Las Golondrinas*, tel 412-5944, has 100 years experience in the business. Its boats make trips, lasting about half an hour, along the quay, to the lighthouse at the end of the harbor.

A boat tour with Las Golondrinas is a fine way to appreciate the size of the port of Barcelona

From the Picasso Museum to the Zoo

The Ribera Quarter, located east of Jaume I Square, is where Palaces were being built for the aristocratic families as early as the twelfth century. The façades of the houses usually do not give a fair indication of the architectural beauty hidden within, and the only way to get a better appreciation of them is to enter the inner courtyards. These ancient palaces usually remained well-preserved for a long time, because when the noblemen left, the families who came instead had the means to care for and preserve the property. Recently, many palaces have been given over to the municipality or other institutions, and they now serve as either museums or public offices.

We reach our point of departure by subway to the Jaume I station, or by bus no. 16, 17, 22, or 45. From Plaça de l'Angel, we turn east on Carrer de la Princesa and then right to the loveliest street in the area, Carrer Montcada, with its two important museums and many prestigious galleries.

At no. 15-19 Montcada Street is the **Picasso Museum** (Museu Picasso) located in exquisite Gothic palaces from the fourteenth century, which were the homes of the noblemen Berenguer d'Aguilar and Baró de Castellet. The museum is open Tues.-Sat. 10am-8pm, Sun. 10am-3pm. Closed on

One of the Gothic palaces that houses the Picasso Museum

Mondays. Tel. 319-6310. There is an entrance fee.

Pablo Ruiz y Picasso was deeply attached to the city of Barcelona. Although he was born in Málaga (in 1881), he was sent at age 14 to study painting in Barcelona. This city was the first stop on his way to conquer the world with his paintbrush. Picasso's special affection for the city found expression even in his lifetime when, at the end of the 1960's, he donated tens of his oil paintings and hundreds of his sketches to the museum. His faithful secretary Sabartés, a native son of Barcelona, also donated some of Picasso's works and, after his death, so did his widow Jacqueline. The result is that this museum has become one of the most important for admirers of Picasso and for those wishing to familiarize themselves with the broad scope of his work.

From the inner court steps, we go up to the first floor to begin our tour. In the first rooms we see a very extensive collection of ceramic works, plates, bowls, and vases, decorated by Picasso, in the 40's, 50's and 60's.

In room no. 4 works from his childhood and youth (1891-1895) are exhibited. Of special interest, are two tambourines. Picasso painted, on the stretched skin of the tambourines a bearded man and an old woman reading. Next to these are Picasso's sketchbook and books in whose margins he "scribbled" and signed his name.

In room no. 5 is an exciting series of paintings, oil on canvas, which Picasso painted in Barcelona in 1896-1897,

Charming little shops on a quiet street by the Picasso Museum

The waiting crowds, enthusiastic to peek at the wonders Picasso performed with his paintbrush

three self-portraits, and portraits of his father, José Ruiz Picasso and his mother, Maria Lopez. In rooms 7 and 8 are more works from the period of his stay in

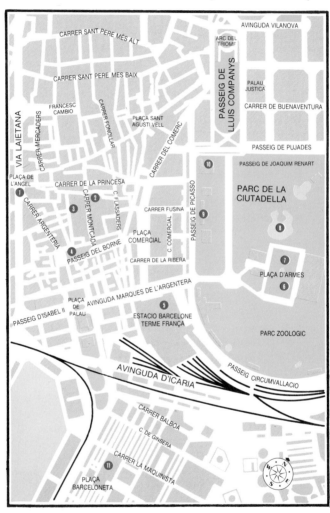

FROM THE PICASSO MUSEUM TO THE ZOO

1. Picasso Museum
2. Museum of Textile and Clothing
3. Santa Maria del Mar Church
4. França Train Station
5. Parliament
6. Museum of Modern Art
7. The park's fountain
8. Geology Museum
9. Zoological Museum
10. La Barceloneta

Barcelona, small oil paintings on wood, and work that he did in school, "anatomical" paintings and sketches of the male body. In room no. 9 a work that Picasso painted when he was only 15 years old, catches the eye – a portrait of aunt Pepa

Cycling at the Parc de la Ciutadella

(Retrat de la Tia Pepa), a powerful work, especially admirable considering his age at the time. Another, more famous work from the same period, which is exhibited in room no. 10 is Science and Charity (Ciéncia Icaritat).

On the second floor of the museum, childhood and youth are left behind. Picasso arrives in Paris (room 16), the year is 1900 and, in his sketches and paintings, can-can dancers and prostitutes from the streets of Pigalle begin to appear. In this room, don't miss one of the more delightful works from this period: the young woman *La Nana*, from 1901, a patchwork of colors and a countenance not quickly forgotten. In rooms 17 and 18 are works from the Blue Period (*Epoca Blava*), 1901-1904, in which the blue hues indeed dominate the pastel drawings, the oils, and the aquarelles. In room 19, among other things, is one of Picasso's most famous works, the Harlequin (*L'Arlquin*), from 1917, which he painted in Barcelona. There are also good examples of Picasso's Cubism, such as the painting of the woman sitting in a chair (*Dona en una Butaca*).

Strolling along, enjoying the exquisitely angled buildings

In rooms 20 and 21 we have the entire series of *Les Menines*, one of the most important and famous among this museum's collection. In these paintings, Picasso imparted his own personal meaning to the famous painting of Velázquez, which is found today in the Prado in Madrid. The entire series

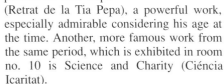

was painted in 1957 in Picasso's studio in the city of Cannes. From the same period, in the next room, we see paintings of doves (*Els Colomins*) and an oil portrait on canvas of his wife, Jacqueline.

In room 27, hang a row of 26 sketches of scenes from the bullfighting arena (*La Tauromaquia*) and similar works etched in copper. In the adjacent rooms are lithographs by Picasso (again from the famous series of "Doves"), engravings, aquatints, and other works of art.

At the lovely Textile and Clothing Museum

On the ground floor of the museum is a pleasant cafeteria, where you can relax, have a drink, or eat a meal (between 12 noon and 4pm: a little expensive). Alongside, is a souvenir shop with reproductions, postcards, books, Picasso-shirts, Picasso-bags, etc.

As you leave the Picasso Museum, almost opposite it, in 12-14 Montcada, you find a very different museum, the **Museum of Textile and Clothing** (Museu Tèxtil i d'Indumentària). It is open Tues.-Sat. 10am-5pm. Tel. 310-4516, on Sundays 9am-2pm, closed on Mondays. There is an entrance fee.

In a palace from the fourteenth century, which belonged to the family of the Marqués de Llió, the history of clothing and its various accessories from the sixteenth until the first half of the twentieth century is depicted. This museum gains its raison d'etre from the fact that, historically, Barcelona is an important textile center. On the ground floor is an extensive collection of embroidery and delicate lace work, tablecloths, curtains, scarves, and fans. On the second floor is an assortment of dresses of noblewomen, hats, gloves, stockings, corsets, hairpins, bone combs, cosmetic kits, purses, and even flasks of smelling salts, in the event that any of them fainted.

The elegant ballroom gowns of the nineteenth century, with their bustles, padded with pillows, and the "new wave" feminist dresses of 1900-1920 are eye-catching. In one of the rooms are ancient weaving looms, spindles and old sewing machines.

Santa Maria del Mar Church – a beautiful example of the local Gothic style

We return to Montcada Street. At no. 20, behind mighty wooden doors, you'll find the lovely courtyard of **Palau Dalmases**. During the day, the yard is open, and it is possible to enter and look at the staircase with its two carved stone arches. Adjacent, at house no. 22, is a delightful café, whose interior is decorated with painted ceramic tiles, where you can relax and have something to drink.

Emerging from the street, a glance to the right reveals the massive outlines of the **Santa Maria del Mar Church**, from the first half of the fourteenth century. It is one of the better examples of the local Gothic style. Its interior is impressive, and very clean, with a row of stone pillars which get closer together as they approach the altar. According to historical documents, it was in front of this church that those sentenced during the Inquisition were burnt at the stake. Today, of course, the square is safe for members of all religions. The church is open to the public daily from 10am-12:30pm and 5-8pm. Tel. 310-2390. Don't miss it.

From this church, we go east with

Passeig del Borne to the Plaça Comércial, where we see a high metal building which houses various fairs and exhibitions. To the right of it, at the end of the street, you can see the "French" Train Station (Estació de França), where much of the trade between Spain and France passes. It is conducted on the trains connecting these two countries.

Barcelona locals having a ball

We go to the station and turn left, on the broad Marqués de l'Argentera Street, to reach the entrance to a district which is both beautiful and rich in tourist attractions, the **Parc de la Ciutadella**. When, at the end of the "War of Succession", Philip V captured Barcelona, in September of 1714, he didn't stop at a series of punishments which deprived the Catalonians of any kind of autonomous framework. In 1716, he ordered the construction of a strong military fortress here, in order to keep an eye on the rebellious inhabitants. All the homes in the area were completely destroyed, and thousands of people were banished in order to clear the area for the fortress.

This spiritual and physical scar was erased by the municipal government in 1868, when the fortress was destroyed, and in its place a park was created. A number of attractive buildings were erected in it and, in 1888, it was the scene of the World Fair.

The southeastern part of the park is devoted to the **Municipal Zoo** (Parc Zoologic). It is open every day from 10am until dusk. Tel.

319-8156; for detailed information call Tel. 221-2506. There is an entrance fee and an additional charge for seeing the dolphins perform. This zoo has an important wing of large mammals, predators, and winged creatures brought from Africa. Most are confined as though in their natural habitat, so that it is more pleasant to observe them than if they had been caged behind bars.

In the middle of the park is a rectangular plaza with flower beds and "square" trees, the result of careful, geometric pruning.

Enjoying the lush green of the city park

This is the Plaça d'Armes. Stretching along it is a building, with a tiled roof, most of which serves as the **Catalonian Parliament**. On the left end is the **Museum of Modern Art** (Museu d'Art Modern). It is open Tues.-Sun. from 9am-9:30pm, closed on Mondays. There is an entrance fee.

The "modern art" referred to in the museum's name is somewhat restricted in regard to provenance and period. There is a collection of paintings, sculpture, sketches, prints etc. of Catalonian artists from the nineteenth and early twentieth centuries – among the better known: Casas, Nonell, and Zuloaga – alongside several works of

Salvador Dali and Joan Miró. The musuem also has a section devoted to decorative art, with emphasis placed on Art Nouveau.

If you walk toward the northern part of the park you will find yourself passing by hundreds of trees, brought here from the four corners of the world. Botany enthusiasts will be happy to see the Himalayan cedar, the related Atlas Mountain cedar, the Japanese acacia, the Canary Island palm tree, and many more. At the base of each tree is a sign with its name.

The Arch of Triumph – an impressive relic from the 1888 World Fair

Amidst the trees is a round pool with water fowl splashing about and waiting for crumbs from the tourists. Opposite the pool, stands the huge "stone monster" in neo-classical style. This is the park's fountain, commissioned by the Barcelona municipality at the end of the nineteenth century, and executed by a group of architects, said to include Gaudí, who was then a brilliant student.

In the western corner of the park are two more museums, usually visited only by those especially interested in these subjects. One is the **Geology Museum** (Museu de Geologia), open Tues.-Sun. from 10am-2pm and closed Mondays (entrance fee). Tel. 319-6895.

Written sources note that this is the oldest museum in Barcelona. It was built in 1878, in order to house the collection brought to the city by the geologist Francesc Martorell Peña. Today, it has the most extensive collection of crystals in all of Spain.

The Zoology Museum made to resemble a royal castle

Next to it is the **Zoology Museum** (Museu de Zoologia). It is open Tues.-Sun. from 10am-2pm; closed on Mondays (entrance fee). Tel. 319-6950.

To begin with, take a close look at the building, made to resemble a royal castle, which houses the museum. This is the work of the architect Montaner designed for the 1888 World Fair (originally it was a restaurant). Inside are exhibits of skeletons, stuffed animals, insects, etc.

Opposite the museum, to the northwest, is the beginning of the broad boulevard Passeig de Lluís Companys. Walking along it, we pass the **Palace of Justice** (Palau Justica), seat of Barcelona's courts, until we reach another monumental relic from the Fair, the **Arch of Triumph** (Arc del Triomf).

Nearby sites

La Barceloneta (little Barcelona): south of the Park of the Citadel, in the direction of the sea, on a triangular salient, is the unique and picturesque Barceloneta Quarter. You can go directly there with the subway to the Barceloneta station (the

"yellow" line L4) or by bus lines: 17, 39, 45, 57, 59, 64.

In the eighteenth century, the city's leaders decided to clear this area of its poor hovels and miserable huts and to replace it with a newly built quarter which would be occupied by the previous inhabitants, who were mostly fishermen and port workers. It was an urban-architectural experiment which was daring for its time. When carried out, the experiment resulted in a pattern of precisely lined-up streets and narrow rows of houses, all going from south to north, with the intention of allowing the sea breeze to pass between them and cool the summer nights a bit.

The quarter has remained very much working class, even today, though fewer fishermen and port workers now live there, as compared with the number of factory workers. Yet, Barceloneta is the real center of popular fish restaurants, which offer a selection of the sea's bounty, including shellfish, oysters and clams.

On the southeast edge of Barceloneta, adjacent to the seashore, is the municipal beach of Barcelona, which on sunny days is a great attraction for tourists. On the shore, one next to the other, are fish restaurants, which move their tables down to the water's edge so that you can combine sunbathing and swimming with a good meal, while you listen to the strains of guitars and accordions played by musicians who wander from table to table.

One of the recommended restaurants right on the beach front, at Plaça Sant Miguel, is *La Gaviota*, whose specialty, *Paella*, is simply delicious.

On the western side of Barceloneta lies the

Port Vell Marina. Here, too, you can take a leisurely stroll, or eat in one of the fine restaurants along the port.

Palm trees at the sunny beach near Barceloneta

Eixample – Outside the Walls

In 1860, the walls of the old city of Barcelona were levelled in order to allow the city to expand toward the northwest. The man who originated the project was the engineer and city planner, Idelfons Cerdá. It was he who later gave the district the name, Eixample, meaning development or growth. The plan called for straight streets, parallel to the shoreline, intersected at right angles by others. On a map or from the air, the result resembles a huge checkerboard. An exception to this harmony is the broad boulevard, Av. Diagonal, which, true to its name, runs at a diagonal (for a length of about ten kms!).

This large urban project had the good fortune to be mounted during the period of flourishing "modernism" in Catalonian architecture. The end of the nineteenth and beginning of the twentieth centuries were the years in which public buildings, residences, shops, courtyards, etc. were erected in the quarter, with various trends of the Art Nouveau style predominating. To the traditional building materials, the architects added ceramics, steel, glass – and much imagination and daring. The most well-known of these architects, some of whose work is found in the quarter is, of course, Gaudí. A walk through the quarter will reveal the unique beauty found in the synthesis of architecture and the decorative arts. It will also provide exciting shopping and entertainment possibilities: in its department stores, luxury shops, art galleries, and movie houses, restaurants, and bars. The overall impression is one of elegance.

Plaça de Catalunya in the heart of the city

The starting point for our tour is the illustrious square of Barcelona, the joyful heart of the city, **Plaça de Catalunya**. It is very easy to get to or to get near to from any direction – it is the largest junction in the city: on subway lines L1 (red), L3 (green), on the urban train; and on many buses, including 9, 16, 17, 18, 22, 24, 28, 35, 38, 47, 66, and others.

Feeding pigeons in Plaça de Catalunya

This expansive square is enclosed by very large buildings, mostly the main branches of banks and financial institutions. The most impressive, built in the "Old New York" style, houses the **Banco de Bilbao**. In the northern corner of the square is an interesting statue of Marés: a young woman on a sturdy horse, waving a sailboat over her head; behind her, a man holds the reins of the horse and, in his other hand, is the cogged wheel of a machine. Opposite, is the large **El Corte Inglés** department store. From its cafeteria on the top floor, you can look down for a bird's eye view of the Catalunya Square.

Casa Batlló

Below, you can wander around the square (it is the same size as the Étoile Square in Paris) and observe the play of the water in its two large fountains, flower beds, and lovely statues.

We leave the square for the **Passeig de Gràcia**, the main artery of our route. After a few minutes of walking, we reach an intersection, where we meet up with the city's largest cross-town street, which runs from one end of town to the other, the Gran Vía de les Corts Catalanes. Also notice the

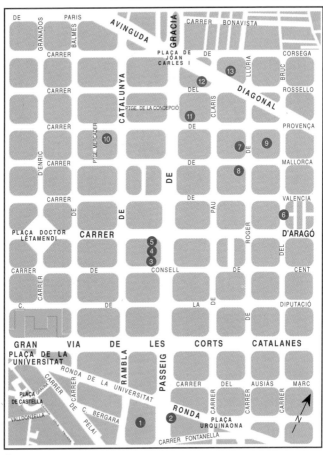

EIXAMPLE

1. Plaça de Catalunya
2. El Corte Inglés
3. The house of Lleó i Morera
4. Casa Amatller
5. Casa Batlló
6. La Concepció Market
7. Palau Casades
8. Casa Montaner
9. Casa Thomas
10. Historical Museum of Medicine
11. Casa Milà
12. Music Museum
13. Casa de les Punxes

lovely street lamps, of cast metal made, in Art Nouveau style, at the beginning of the century, by the artist Pere Falques. On the Gran Vía, near the intersection are two of the most luxurious hotels in the city. A peek into their entrance lobbies affords an interesting view of the classical luxury of times past. Going right from the intersection, we find the *Ritz*, and left of it, the *Avenida Palace*.

Continuing up the Passeig de Gràcia, at the corner of the street (no. 21) is an impressive building, constructed for a branch of the Spanish *Phoenix* company, topped by a dome and, on it, a youth riding on a royal winged creature. At no. 35, also a corner building, is the house of **Lleó i Morera**, one of the noblemen of the city at the end of the nineteenth century, built by the architect Montaner. It has gone through many changes, and the last renovation was completed in 1992. Today it houses, among other things, the Main Municipal Tourist Office. If you have business here, you can also enjoy the rare beauty of this building's interior.

In Barcelona designs, originality is the name of the game – lampposts on Passeig de Gràcia

At no. 39 of this street is the **Perfume Museum** (Museu del Perfume). Open Mon.-Fri from 10:30am-1:30pm and 4:30-8pm, closed on Saturdays and Sunday afternoons. Tel. 216-0146. There is no entrance fee.

In the museum is an exhibit of perfume containers and cosmetic equipment, flasks and bottles, from different historical periods up to the present time. The interesting collection includes ancient Greek ceramics and Roman glass vessels.

Further on, on the same side of the street, at

no. 41, is the neo-Gothic construction of the architect Cadafalch called **Casa Ametller**. Next to it, at no. 43. is a building planned by Gaudí called **Casa Batlló** (see "Gaudí's Barcelona").

The next street we meet up with, walking up the Passeig de Gràcia, is Carrer d'Aragó. If we go left until we reach number 255, we see the first "modernistic" building constructed in Barcelona, built in 1880, by Montaner. Red bricks constitute its façade, with a pointed cornice on top and, on it, a head covered with a metal mask. The row of windows on the second floor, three on each side, is factory-like in appearance. Today, the building houses the museum and library of **Fundació Antoni Tàpies**, Tel. 487-0315. Open Tues.-Sun. from 11am-8pm; closed on Mondays. The museum was opened in 1984 by the Catalan painter Antoni Tàpies to promote the study of modern art and culture. It presents exhibitions of modern art from all over the world.

A fragrant welcome to the charming roofed Concepció Market

Continuing right with d'Aragó Street, we reach the lovely roofed **La Concepció Market**, next to the Gothic church (whose roofed entranceway was erected in the fourteenth century). You can walk through the market and pause in the back section, where you will find fish and seafood stalls, giving off wonderful aromas of salt and fresh fish. Exiting from the other side of the market brings us to Carrer de Valéncia. Left, at the corner, is the **Conservatory of Music** (Escola Municipal de Musica). Its beautiful façade faces the intersection with two conical towers, covered with scaled tiles. This is the work of the architect Antoni de Falguera.

In Eixample – an imaginative synthesis of architecture and decorative art

Further along the street, turning right with Carrer de Roger de Lluria, we reach the intersection of Carrer de Mallorca. Here, there are three architectural creations which are well worth observing in detail. First, at no. 283, is the small but very luxurious palace, **Palau Casades**, which today houses the Barcelona advocates' bureau. At no. 278 is **Casa Montaner**, with an exquisite colored ceramic façade, which today houses the government offices of Catalonia. At no. 291 is **Casa Thomas**, also the work of the architect Montaner. Today, it houses a commercial firm.

We return to the Carrer de Mallorca and walk toward the Passeig de Gràcia, crossing the street, until we come to a small lane which leads off to the right: Passatge Mercader. At house no. 11 is the **Historical Museum of Medicine** (Museu d'História de la Medicina). Open Mon.-Fri. from 10am-1pm. Tel. 216-0500. There is an entrance fee.

In this museum, which should prove to be of

The interior of Casa Milà, an example of Gaudí's original style

interest not only to doctors or patients, we can see a depiction of the evolution of medicine throughout history, by virtue of the 2500 different artefacts on display. Among other things, you can see various possessions that belonged to famous Catalonian medical personages.

Returning to the Passeig de Gràcia, at no. 92 you will find yet another of the famous works of Gaudí, **Casa Milà** (see "Gaudí's Barcelona"). Continuing up the street, we come to Av. Diagonal, and continue along it until we reach no. 373, where the **Music Museum** (Museu de la Musica) is housed. Open from Tues.-Sun. 10am-2pm and 5-8pm. Closed on Mondays. Tel. 416-1157. There is an entrance fee.

In the museum are various musical instruments, arranged according to their origins, from the sixteenth to the twentieth centuries. Next to them is documentary material about well-known Catalonian composers. Note the imposing guitar collection, one of the most

Casa Milà

important in the world. Incidentally, the museum is housed in one of the buildings designed by the architect Cadafalch and was built in 1902 for the Baró de Quadras.

The **Casa de les Punxes**, another large, more luxurious example of the work of the architect Cadafalch, is not far from the museum, at no. 416 on this street. It is an interesting combination of modernism with medieval motifs.

We make our way back toward Plaça de Catalunya via the Rambla de Catalunya, the street parallel to the southwest of the Passeig de Gràcia. It is a pleasant boulevard, not too noisy, with numerous cafés, which move their tables outdoors under the shade of the Rambla's row of birch trees.

A combination of modernism and medieval motifs at Casa de les Punxes

Montjuïc —
The Upper Storey of the City

In the south of the city, stretching from east to west, is Montjuïc Hill, reaching 210 meters above sea level. It's name, which means "Mountain of the Jews", is derived from the Jewish cemetery which used to be on the mountain during medieval times. Today, most of the cemetery relics are found in the City History Museum (see "the Gothic Quarter"). Only near the end of the nineteenth century was the hill annexed to the Barcelona municipality. Jean-Claude Forestier, the French garden landscape artist, was asked to design gardens and beauty spots in the area. The project was executed by the local architect Rubió i Tudur.

The "International Exhibition" of 1929 brought with it a wave of construction and development to Barcelona, which helped determine the character of Montjuïc and gave it prominence. Most of the buildings and the landscape design of today had their origins in the preparations for that exhibition.

The "Exhibition Towers", welcoming the visitors to the area of the "Barcelona Fair"

We begin our tour in the large **Plaça d'Espanya**, which is actually the entrance to the "exhibition" site. You can reach the spot by subway to the Espanya station (lines L1, L3) or by bus on one of the lines: 9, 27, 38, 50, 56, 109. The climb up the mountain, via the winding roads, is not always easy (this is a relative matter, of course, and depends on your strength);

you can take bus no. 61, which leaves from Espanya Square, passes by most of the tourist sites, and reaches the highest point, near the military museum.

Another possibility for ascending the mountain is to take the cablecar (*funicular*), which leaves from the Paral-Lel subway station (line L3), and then to continue on the *telefèric* cablecar.

The last possibility, which also includes an imposing view of the harbor and of the entire city, is to go up the mountain via another cablecar, the one which leaves from the port. Tickets to the cablecar can be purchased at the kiosk at the left end of Portal de la Pau Square. Then proceed to one of the high metal towers. Use either the short route or the longer one to get to the various places on the hill.

An enchanting vision – a night scene in Montjuïc

There are many exhibitions and fairs in the area of Montjuïc, throughout the year. You should take into consideration that when these events occur, the routine life in the area is affected, buslines stop or change their routes, and entrance to the area is restricted to those with entrance tickets. In that event, go around the "fair", to the right or left via any of the streets.

By one route or another, we have reached Espanya Square. In its center is a monumental fountain. On the north is a round structure, the city's old bull ring, Plaça de Toros les Arenes (not functioning in recent years). On the south there are two towers, slightly strange in appearance, made of red bricks, 47 meters high, topped by a

"Greek temple" with a pyramid on top of that. These are the **"Exhibition Towers"** (Torres de l'Exposició), the gateway to the

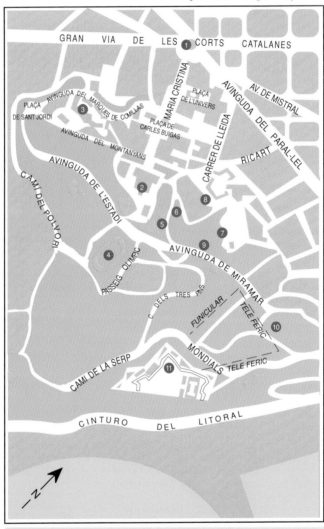

MONTJUÏC

1. Plaça d'Espanya
2. National Palace
3. Poble Espanyol
4. Olympic Stadium
5. Albéniz Palace
6. Ethnological Museum
7. Greek Theater
8. Archaeological Museum
9. Joan Miró Foundation
10. Amusement Park of Motjuïc
11. Montjuïc Castle

area of the "Barcelona Fair" (Fira de Barcelona), an area of 25,000 sq/m., used today for large exhibitions on a variety of subjects. Some of the fair buildings previously belonged to the "International Exhibition" of 1929. Avinguda de la Reina Maria Cristina is a boulevard surrounded by greenery and pools with water fountains. It leads to the grand fountain, pride of the city, built by the architect Carles Buigas. This fountain presents an astounding play of water and colored lights – up to fifty different shades. You can view the display: in winter, on Sat. and Sun. from 8pm-11pm (the musical accompaniment is only between 9pm-10pm); in summer, on Thurs. Sat. and Sun. from 9pm-12 midnight (musical accompaniment is only between 10-11pm).

Above, are steps leading to a massive structure, with a large dome in the middle and two smaller domes in the corners. It is the **National Palace** (Palau Nacional). It, too, was built in 1929, and it houses the **Museum of Art of Catalonia** (Museu d'Art de Catalunya) which has a vast art library and an important collection of drawings, engravings, stamps and coins. Open Tues.-

The "Exhibition Towers" – their name gives a clue as to their function

Sun. from 9am-2pm; closed Tuesdays. tel. 423-1824. There is an entrance fee; no admission fee on Sundays.

Many people think that the Romanesque and Gothic collections in this museum are among the most important in the world. The wealth of art works, and it should be added, the imposing manner in which they are displayed in its approximately 70 display rooms, arouses much admiration.

From the large entrance hall, turn right to the Romanesque wing, which has works from the eleventh to thirteenth centuries. Remnants of wall paintings (frescos) of great beauty have been brought here from churches and monasteries, which were destroyed – in Catalonia, the Pyrenean valleys and throughout Spain. Builders of the museum devised round chapel niches and halls resembling the interiors of churches, in order to preserve the effect created by them in their original surroundings. Complementing the period pieces are wooden sculptures from the twelfth and thir-

teenth centuries and church furnishings with carvings, occasionally, of Byzantine influence. Especially beautiful is a piece of furniture from the twelfth century – three adjacent seats, of walnut wood, with a decorated canopy. The arrangement of the exhibit is such that you can follow the artistic development of a particular subject. For example, there is a comprehensive series of wooden statues of the "Virgin and Child", showing the evolution of carving styles in various shades of color.

From this section, a stairway leads to the second floor, where there is a special section devoted to ceramic works. Here, in a long

The National Palace, built in 1929, houses the Museum of Art of Catalonia

row of rooms, is an extensive collection from ancient periods; from the Arab period, the Middle Ages, and later periods, from Spain and elsewhere in Europe. The exhibit includes large jugs, vases, pitchers, plates, bowls, figures of animals, and painted tiles. The tremendous wealth of colors has been preserved, despite the venerable age of the objects: the blue is still strong, the green verdant, and the red full of depth and warmth. In room no. 9 of the ceramic section there is an interesting collection of painted wall tiles, depicting scenes from daily life, artisans at work, hunters, warriors, musicians – all tending to the humorous or even to the grotesque. Here is folk art at its best.

Another series of wall tiles, using what would today be described as "comic book" technique, depicts scenes from the New Testament. In room no. 7 are scenes from the life of the city of Barcelona in the seventeenth and eighteenth centuries. In room no. 4 are large and impressive eating utensils, which were used in the royal household and among the aristocratic families.

The Museum of Art of Catalonia contains a tremendously rich collection of art work

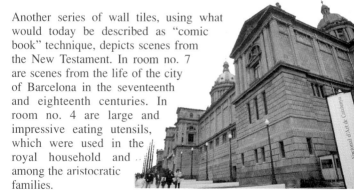

Poble Espanyol – a life size exhibition of building styles found in the different parts of Spain

We go back down to the ground floor, to the entrance hall, and cross over to the left side of the hall to the Gothic art section. The collection in this wing faithfully represents the art of the fourteenth and fifteenth centuries, of Catalonia in particular, but, also that of other parts of Spain, such as Aragon and Seville. In the various rooms are triptychs describing scenes from the lives of the saints, religious objects, chalices, decorated crucifixes, incense boxes – all made of wood, precious metals, and ivory. The sculptures of a local artist from the fourteenth century, Jaume Cascalls de Berga, are of outstanding beauty. At the end of the wing, we hop to the sixteenth and seventeenth centuries, to the works of Spanish, Italian, and Flemish artists like El Greco, Tintoretto, and Viladomat.

From the expanse in front of the museum a stairway leads left to the Passeig de les Cascadas, to a path that goes through the botanical garden toward the peripheral road of the mountain, which, at this section (the names change) is called Avinguda del Marques de Comillas. We go left with this road and come to one of the well-known and colorful landmarks of Barcelona: the **Poble Espanyol** (the Spanish village)..

The **Poble Espanyol** (tel. 325-7866) was also built especially for the "International Exhibition" of 1929 and was left in place, to become an attraction for visitors to the city. It is actually an architectural exhibition, life-size, of the styles of construction in the different provinces of Spain – its villages and cities – public buildings, private homes, and streets, stairways, squares, cafés, restaurants, and shops set out in an area of 5 acres. All together, it creates a lovely mosaic, which, were it not real, could exist only in one's imagination.

Of course, such a "gimmick" cannot avoid a very high degree of commercialism, so visitors are "attacked" on all sides by souvenir shops, stalls selling jewelry, clothing, prints, glassware, Spanish guitars – and what not? There is also a bank branch where you can exchange money and a tourist bureau (to the right of the entrance gate). In the broad central expanse, Plaza Mayor, an orchestra plays for the enjoyment of passersby. In the evenings, night clubs, cabarets, bars, etc. are open.

All you need do (and should do) is wander through the streets, look up at the buildings,

The Poble Espanyol was built especially for the "International Exhibition" which took place in 1929

The Olympic Stadium of Barcelona, host of the Twenty Fifth Olympic Games

and imagine yourself travelling from place to place in Spain: Saragossa, Segovia, Toledo, Guadalajara, Cádiz, Tarragona, and even...Barcelona.

When we leave Poble Espanyol, we turn right and return the way we came to the National Palace. We can also (on foot or by bus no. 61) turn left on Avinguda de l'Estadi, which changes direction and goes around the hill, passing various sports facilities, until it reaches a spot above the National Palace. On the right is the **Olympic Stadium** of Barcelona (Estadi Olímpic). It first opened its gates in 1929 and has 80,000 seats. Here, the opening and closing ceremonies of the Twenty-Fifth Olympic Games took place, in 1992. Near the southern gate of the stadium (Port La Sud) stands the **Olympic Gallery** (Galeria Olímpica) dedicated to the Olympic Games in Barcelona. It

Gold, silver and bronze – the aspiration of every sportsman

includes an archive of photograph and videotapes, a reading room open to the public with videos, photographs, publications and other material concerning the games (open Tues.-Fri., prior booking necessary) and an Auditorium, where lectures and daily audiovisual presentations regarding the 1992 games and Olympic games in general are shown. The gallery is open Tues.-Sat. from 10am-2pm and 4-8pm, Sun. and holidays 10am-2pm. Closed on Mondays. Tel. 426-0660. There is an entrance fee.

Not far from the Olympic Gallery is the **Albéniz Palace** (Palau Albeniz), which, in 1929, served as the royal guesthouse of the "International Exhibition" and, today, is the venue of festive municipal receptions. On Sundays, those who wish to can walk through the beautiful gardens of the palace, **Jardins J. Maragall**.

North of the palace, a winding road (Passeig de Santa Madrona) leads down between three interesting sites: the Ethnological Museum, the "Greek Theater", and the Archeological Museum. Those who prefer to return in the direction of the National Palace, following the visit to Poble Espanyol, can tour these three sites from the opposite direction, until they find themselves climbing up the hill.

It is only natural that there should be an **Ethnological Museum** (Museu Etnologic) in a city like Barcelona, from whose port many sailors have set sail for distant lands and different cultures and returned home laden with souvenirs. The museum is open Tues.-Sat. from 9am-8:30pm, on Sundays from 9am-2pm, Mondays 2-8:30pm. Tel. 424-6402. There is an entrance fee.

The museum exhibits show the cultural development of different groups of people in their arts, religion, and daily life. The rich permanent exhibits have come from the countries of Latin America, Asia, Africa, and Oceania. There are colorful masks, wooden and stone sculptures, folkart, and more. The museum also has temporary exhibits on various subjects.

Continuing on our way, a stairway leads to a

At the Olympic Village in Montjuïc

well-tended garden whose beds are precisely laid out and whose trees are pruned geometrically. It is located at the entrance of what is referred to as the "**Greek Theater**" (Teatre Grec). It was given this name because it represents a replica of an ancient Greek theater, built on the former site of a stone quarry. Its semicircular seating plan has place for 2000 people, around a circular stage. In this open air theater, in the summer, there are many performances of music, dance, etc.

Returning to our route, we can see, on the left, at a bend in the road, another imposing structure from the "Exhibition" that in 1929 was a palace of graphic arts and today is the home of the **Archaeological Museum** (Museu Arqueológic). It is open Tues.-Sat. from 10am-5pm (on Tues. and Thurs. 10am-7pm). Tel. 423-2149; 423-5601. Closed on Mondays. There is an entrance fee.

The open-air "Greek Theater" which hosts many performances in the summer

The museum possesses many artefacts documenting different aspects of man's activity, starting from the paleolithic period (the early stone age) until the age of the Visigoths. Most of the objects are taken from excavations made in Catalonia, the Costa Brava, and the Balearic Islands. Impressive work has been done in this museum in

The Joan Miró Foundation, devoted to the great Catalonian artist

making reproductions of art objects, mosaics, etc. from ancient Greece and from the Roman empire.

From here, we return to the main road of Montjuïc, whose name changes, to the Avinguda de Miramar, at the intersection with Passeig Santa Madrona. We take this street left and notice a modern white building. This is the **Joan Miró Foundation** (Fundació Joan Miró), a center devoted to the outstanding Catalonian artist, to research and to exhibitions of contemporary artists. It is open Tues.-Sat. from 11am-7pm, Sundays and holidays 10:30am-2:30pm, closed on Mondays. Tel. 329-1908. There is an entrance fee.

The cornerstone of the Miró Foundation was laid by the artist himself in 1971 with a dual purpose in mind: to exhibit the works of Miró and to promote his art by means of research projects, special events and other activities, so as to encourage and publicize, generally, different aspects of contemporary art. Within

Miramar →
← Anella Olímpica
← Inefc
← Fundació Joan Miró
Parc d'Atraccions →
Castell →

The Joan Miró Foundation owns a very large collection of the artist's works, therefore exhibits sometimes alternate

this framework, temporary exhibits are held here, as well as concerts of modern music, video evenings, gatherings, etc.

The building, whose doors were opened to the public in June 1975, was designed by the famous architect Josep Lluís Sert, a personal friend of Miró. Sert, who was for many years the president of the International Congress of Modern Architecture, is one of the renowned artists in this field in the present century. Among his better known works are the Spanish pavillion of the International Exhibition of Paris of 1937, the American Embassy in Baghdad, and the plan for the presidential palace in the Hague (which was never executed). In the Montjuïc project, he attempted to see through Miró's eyes, with the intention of creating a suitable "container" for the works of the artist he admired so much.

Inside this unique building, a right turn in the entrance hall will lead you to where the tour begins. The first room offers photographs of biographical landmarks in the life of Miró – his birth in Barcelona on April 20, 1893, family photos, the earliest drawing of his in the museum, made when he was 8 years old, a marvelous sketch of a peacock, drawn when he was 14, and more.

The route passes among various works of Miró the painter, the engraver, the sculptor, and the artistic innovator; Miró the surrealist, the imaginative, dynamic, multifaceted, artist whose words were full of humor. In the second room, there is a huge wall carpet from 1979 called *Llana* (wool), which was especially made for this museum and, next to it – a creation with eight umbrellas, from 1973 (*Sobreteixim*). On the second floor, the eye is caught by one of Miró's famous works, *Sun Bird* from 1968, done in white Carrara marble. Further along, there are also interesting photo portraits of Miró, made by some of the most famous photographers of our time, including Man Ray and Irving Penn.

One of the museum's most important collections is a series of engravings called *Série Barcelone* (Barcelona Series), from the years 1939-1944. This museum is the only place in the world which possesses the entire series of 50 prints in black and white (each produced in only five copies), considered to be one of the most imposing artistic documentations of the Spanish civil war.

*Montjuïc by night –
A variety of colors
and lights*

It should be noted that the number of Miró's works in the possession of this museum is very large. There are 217 paintings, 153 sculptures, nine textile art works, all the prints he ever made in his entire life, and about 5000 sketches and preparatory designs for various works. The impressive scope obliges the curators to alternate exhibits, so that some of Miró's works are on display part of the time and, at other times, they are stored in the basement. During the summer when there are numerous visitors, the museum puts as many works as possible on display. More than 150,000 admirers of Miró visit the museum each year.

Fun up high – at the Amusement Park of Montjuïc

Many of them also enjoy the very elegant restaurant-bar, located on the ground floor (excellent sandwiches or full meals), as well as the shop which sells reproductions, books, and souvenirs.

When we leave the Miró Museum, we turn left on Avinguda de Miramar and reach the southwestern part of the mountain, which overlooks the sea. A wealth of beautiful gardens, beauty spots, statues and observation points make this a very popular place for Barcelona citizens (on weekends), as well as for tourists. The most beautiful observation point, with a wide view of the harbor and the sea, is located at a place called Plaça del Mirador, opposite the entrance to the large **Amusement Park of Montjuïc** (Parc d'Atracciones de Montjuïc). Tel. 441-7024 (Sep. 15-Mar. 3, weekends only, 11:30pm-8pm; April 1-June 20, weekends only, 12 noon-10pm; June 21-Sep. 14, weekdays only, 6-12pm; Fri.-Sat., 6pm-1am; Sun. and holidays 12 noon-11:15pm). This park is full of all the usual popular attractions, from a ghost train to a giant Ferris wheel, with shooting galleries, and carousels for children.

Sentinels on guard at the Military Museum

As we have already mentioned, whoever decides to forgo this part of the walk can take a shortcut, using the cablecar which goes up to the park from the station in the middle of Avinguda de Miramar. It continues on afterwards to the final station at Montjuïc castle. The funicular which leaves from the station next to the cablecar, goes straight up to the castle, the highest point on the hill, and the end of our tour.

The massive Montjuïc Castle, now home of the Military Museum

Today, the imposing **Montjuïc Castle** (Castell de Montjuïc) houses the **Military Museum** (Museu Militar). It is open Tues.-Sun. from 9:30pm-2pm and 3:30-8pm. Closed on Mondays. There is an entrance fee. Tel. 456-6400. This spot served for hundreds of years as a lookout point toward the sea, to keep an eye out for enemies. A large fortress was built here in the eighteenth century, an impressive example of the military architecture of that time. In 1960,

Cannons brought from battlefields – in the castle's inner courtyard

the fortress was transferred to the jurisdiction of the municipality and became a museum. Thick stone walls greet the visitor, as well as a suspended chain bridge over a deep protective moat which, in times past, was filled with water and served as an obstacle against attack. Today, it has flowers growing in it.

In the square inner courtyard of the castle cannons which were brought from battlefields of the near and distant past are on display. A stairway at the western side of the courtyard leads up to the castle roof, from which there is a good view of the surroundings and of the castle trenches, emplacements, and fortifications. In some of the positions, large shore battery cannons are still in place, as if to threaten any enemy ship which might dare to approach the city's harbor.

The military history of Spain is given full coverage in the various rooms of this museum, together with a few pointers concerning other armies near and far. The collections are divided according to subjects and periods. There are swords and bows and arrows from ancient times, medieval armor of the knights, the famous Spanish spear with its double edge, arbalests with metal arrows, etc. Further on, is a large collection of the earliest rifles and pistols, and a display of the development of gun-powder weapons, both local and foreign. Upon seeing the helmets with sharp projections on their sides, the visitor is reminded of events from Spanish military history, involving the Indians of South and Central America, during the Spanish conquest.

In addition, on display in the museum are ancient weapons, helmets, armor, swords and daggers of the Arab armies which conquered Spain, and artefacts from all over the

Barcelona's Military Museum, portraying Spain's long history of wars

The Montjuïc Castle served for years as a lookout point towards the sea

world: Japan, Persia, Chili, India, and the Philippines.

Other sections are devoted to military uniforms, models of ancient fortresses, models of ships and airplanes; entire armies of lead soldiers are used to reconstruct famous historical battles. There are also many drawings and paintings depicting heroic events from Spanish military history.

The museum also houses an exhibition of remains from the Jewish Quarter (Barrio Judio), which was destroyed in 1391.

Montjuïc Hill abounds with lovely well-tended gardens

Pedralbes – the Palace and the Monastery

The Pedralbes Quarter in the western part of the city is a wealthy residential district, which was recently constructed, comprising modern neighborhoods and villas of different styles. The builders took care to preserve a high quality of life, with attractive landscapes and open spaces. The new campus of the **University of Barcelona** is located on Av. Diagonal: the faculties of philosophy and literature, history, sciences, pharmacy, etc. and several colleges including the Sant Jordi School of the Arts are here. To the east, is one of the most luxurious hotels in Barcelona, the *Princesa Sofía*, whose spacious halls host numerous ceremonies and receptions.

To reach the quarter, take a subway to the Palau Reial station (green line L3) or by buses 6, 7, 16, 59, 66, 72, 74, 75.

The exit from the subway station is just opposite the entrance to the garden of the **Pedralbes Palace** (Palau de Pedralbes). The palace was built between 1919-1929 for King Alfonso XIII, the grandfather of the present king, Juan Carlos. But he did not have much opportunity to use the palace, as he was forced to leave Spain in 1931 in order to avoid civil war (see "Introduction – History").

The Italian Renaissance styled Pedralbes Palace, built as residence for king Alfonso XIII

What is called a palace is in fact a pleasant

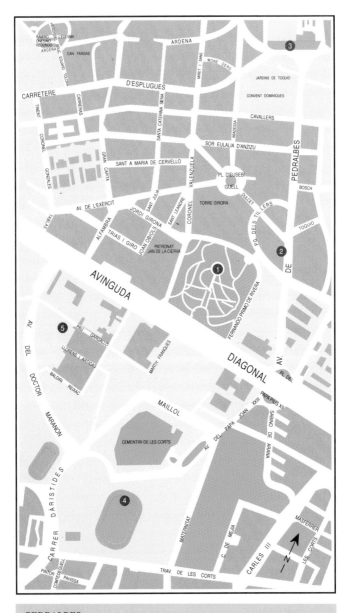

PEDRALBES

1. Pedralbes Palace
2. Pavellons de la Finca Güell
3. Pedralbes Monastery
4. Museum of the Barcelona
   Football Club

summer house in Italian Renaissance style, surrounded by a beautiful garden, a lovely place to take a quiet walk. Immediately after entering the main gate, you encounter a pool whose waters flow down a graded waterfall toward a white marble statue of a beautiful young woman. The garden paths pass between numerous trees, including soaring cedars, and geometrically designed flowerbeds. In various corners there are statues and large decorated stone urns. A little before reaching the expanse at the front of the palace, on the left, hidden in a clump of reeds, is the **Gaudí fountain**, whose metal base is designed in a style which immediately signifies its creater. Next to it is another pool, with flowering water lilies and goldfish.

Serenity reigns supreme – the garden of the palace

Also, in the open space in front of the palace, in a semi-circle framed by a stone balustrade, a pool nestles, surrounded on all sides by potted plants. Above it looms the broad shape of the palace, whose honey-colored walls are decorated with various paintings. On the left is the entrance to the museum of the palace. It is open Tues.-Fri. from 10am-1pm and 4-6pm, and on Saturday and Sunday from 10am-1:30pm; Closed Mondays. There is an entrance fee.

The garden of the Pedralbes Palace – a perfect place for a quiet walk

The palace also houses the **Ceramics Museum** (Museu de Ceramica), with beautiful examples of Catalan and Arabian pottery, Spanish ceramics, etc. A special room is dedicated to contemporary works. Tel. 280-1621.

A walk through the museum will reveal the lovely salons in the palace. In keeping with the architectural structure, they are decorated in Italian Renaissance style. The exhibit includes antique furniture, precious objects, rugs, paintings, and sculpture. On display in glass cabinets are a series of various items which belonged to Spanish kings. Painted portraits of these kings have been hung in a special gallery.

As we leave, from the same main gate of the garden, we go left on Av. Diagonal, passing the Faculty of Law building and turn left again on Av. de Pedralbes. At no. 7 is another of Gaudí's architectonic works, the **Pavellons de la Finca Güell**, built between 1884-1887. This unique structure was meant for the use of the gateman of the Pedralbes Palace and for the palace stables. Today, the building houses the Gaudí cathedra of the

Pedralbes Monastery, one of Barcelona's beautiful spots

College of Architecture of the Barcelona Polytechnic (for details see "Gaudí's Barcelona"). A little further on, on the left, is a new residential neighborhood, built in the style of British cottages.

The road ends in a square and, on the far right, is a narrow street which passes beneath a small stone arch. From here, we enter the **Pedralbes Monastery** (Monestir de Pedralbes), 9 Baixada del Monestir. One of the most beautiful and interesting sites in Barcelona. It is open Tues.-Sun. from 9:30am-2pm, closed on Mondays. Tel. 280-1434. No cameras, umbrellas canes or large handbags are allowed. Metro 1-3; buses 22, 63, 64, 75, 114, BC, BI, SJ. There is an entrance fee. Free entrance on Sundays (exhibition not included).

The monastery was founded in 1326 by Queen Elisenda de Montcada, the wife of Jaume II, King of Aragón and Catalonia. It is built in a distinct Catalonian-Gothic style. Several nuns still live here, in a wing separate from the sections which are open to the public.

A stone gate at the Pedralbes Quarter

In the Sant-Miquel Chapel of the monastery, you can see the famous wall paintings of Ferrer Bassa, from 1346, depicting scenes from the life of Jesus, beginning with his birth, until his crucifixion. The courtyard of the monastery is truly exquisite, built in a large rectangle, enclosed on all sides by three storeys and two rows of delicately designed stone arches (26 pillars in each row). In the middle of the yard is a flowering orchard of fruit trees.

A walk around the yard will allow you a glimpse at a way of life, which always arouses curiosity: monastery life. You can visit the cells, which were designed for prayer and solitude: each has a small opening for the delivery and removal of food and waste.

The monastery hosts the Thyssen-Bornemisza collection of Medieval Art, Germanic Renaissance, Italian Renaissance and Late Venetian Baroque – in all, there are 72 paintings and 8 sculptures by Fra Angelico, Tiziano, Velázquez, Rubens, and others.

The delicately designed stone arches surrounding the courtyard of the Pedralbes Monastery

The dispensary has on display various potions, medicinal plants, and wondrous powders. In the large dining-room used by the nuns, on stone tables, eating utensils are arranged, dishes, bowls, and tableware made of wood. In the kitchen, you can see the cooking utensils, the old meat-grinding machine, and the storehouse, with its large jars, embedded in the earth, to retain the cold.

The simple monastic way of life stands out even more prominently in the nuns' rooms: the beds, the cupboards, all unbelievably bare. It is also interesting to visit the monastery's sick rooms, since one of its functions in the past was to serve as a hospital. Under the beds there are still porcelain bed pans, which were used by the patients. Through the windows, you can see the outer courtyard of the monastery, with its beds of vegetables, grown by the sisters for their own use.

On the right, before the exit from the courtyard, is a room with a collection of various relics from the monastery's past: holy objects and works of art, including a chest made of walnut with ivory decoration from the sixteenth century, intended to hold the possessions of a bride in preparation for her wedding. In the center of the room is a wooden model of the monastery.

Suggestion: You can combine the tours called "Pedralbes" and "Tibidabo" into one trip. Begin in Pedralbes and, when you have finished your visit to the monastery, turn left and walk up the street to the **Plaça de Pedralbes** nearby. From there, bus 22 will take you to John F. Kennedy Square, where there is a station of the "Blue Tram" which goes up to Tibidabo.

Nearby sites

The **Museum of the Barcelona Football Club** (Museu del Fútbol Club Barcelona) south of the Palau Reial subway station, is one of the most popular places in the city.

A holy atmosphere in the chapel of the Pedralbes Monastery

Football fans from Barcelona and from throughout Europe are familiar with the impressive stadium which has hosted so many exciting games. In the stadium, you will also find a museum dedicated to the football team (You can come here directly on bus no. 75).

The museum is open Nov.-March on Tues.-Fri. from 10am-1pm and 4-6pm, on Sat. and Sun. mornings only, closed on Mondays. From April-September, the museum is open Mon.-Sat. from 10am-1pm and 4-7pm. Closed on Sundays. There is an entrance fee. Tel. 330-9411.

In the museum is a collection of trophies and medals awarded to the team, paintings, photos, and souvenirs of their glorious victories. There is also an auditorium where you can see an audiovisual performance about the history of the club. The visit includes a view of the giant stadium from the presidential grandstand.

Living modestly – at the Pedralbes Monastery

Tibidabo – above all

High in the northwest part of the city, from a distance, we see the Tibidabo summit, the best observation point both for viewing Barcelona and the interior of the country. At night, the church at the top is illuminated, serving as a land beacon for those trying to find their bearings. Visitors who love beautiful panoramas should not forgo the climb to the top. The route is lovely and there are interesting sites on the way.

The easiest way to reach this spot from the center of the city is to go to the Plaça de Catalunya station and take the train called Ferrocarril de la Generalitat to the last station, Av. del Tibidabo, beneath the John F. Kennedy Square. At the corner, where the street and the square meet, opposite the subway exit is the beginning of the "Blue Tram" (**Tramvia Blau**), without doubt one of the most entertaining curiosities in the city's public transportation system. It is an electric streetcar from the beginning of the century. This short line was left mainly as a last remaining vestige and reminder of earlier days. Sitting on the streetcar's old wooden benches and listening to the veteran "conductor" greet the passersby, most of whom he is personally acquainted with, makes this trip an experience in itself.

The "Blue Tram" chugs and rattles as it climbs along its winding way between the colorful villas of the quarter, until it reaches its destination, half way up the hill, the square from which the small mountain train, the *Funicular*, sets off to the summit. The train departs every half hour, and in six minutes it reaches the top of Tibidabo (we recommend that you buy return tickets, which are less expensive).

When we leave the train at the upper station, we find ourselves in a square at a

Climbing up Tibidabo in the "Blue Tram" is an experience you should not miss when visiting Barcelona

height of 500 meters above sea level. By making a half-turn to the left at the exit of the observation platform, from this height we have a glorious panoramic view of all Barcelona, including the shoreline and the harbor.

On the right side of the square is hotel *La Masia* which has a restaurant and bar. Though many tourists frequent the place, the service is not the best.

At the Tibidabo Quarter

Opposite, rises the **Sacred Heart of Jesus Church** (Templo Expiatorion del Sagrado Corazo). Tel. 455-0247; It is open from 9am-9pm in June-Aug., until 6pm in the winter. A neo-Gothic building, erected at the beginning of the present century. At the top of the church is a huge statue of Jesus, his arms extended sideways. The front steps lead to a small prayer hall, and from here (in the far left corner) is a passageway to an elevator which takes you (there is a charge) to the roof balcony, for a view at a height of exactly 538.78 meters! But you can definitely make do with a climb to the middle balcony by using the steps found to the right and left of the building. From here, you can also see a panorama of the city, and on clear days, the lovely landscape of the interior of the country as well. Don't miss it. The only thing which slightly "spoils" the view from the church is the television relay antenna which is pitched at its side.

To the right of the station is the entrance gate to the well-known **Amusement Park of Tibidabo**, where there are a great number of rides located at different elevations on the edge of the slope. In the park, there is also a satisfactory self-service restaurant for visitors. In addition to the more-or-less standard attractions of an amusement park (an exception is the "light plane", which is an interesting carousel that exploits the altitude in order to circle over the depths below), there is also an **Automat Museum** (Museu d'Autómats). It is open during the same hours as the amusement park (the entrance fee to the park also includes a visit to the museum): from April to September, daily 11am-8pm, from Oct. to March, Sat. and Sun. only, from 11am-8pm. Tel. 211-7942.

For brave people only – a flight in the "light plane" circling over the depths

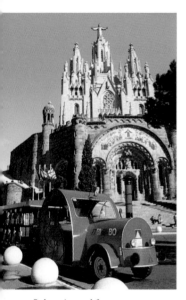

Solemnity and fun – from the Sacred Heart of Jesus Church to the Amusement Park

As its name implies, the museum is devoted to various interesting machines, "robots" widely used in the nineteenth century for the amusement of the rich and the aristocracy, since only they could afford such expensive toys. Even today, these mechanical forms of people and animals evoke a smile of amusement.

Nearby Sites

The **Torre de Collserola** (Collserola Tower) is located on the Turó de la Vilana, on the Collserola ridge, at a height of 445m above sea level. The structure's 13 platforms rise to a total of 288m. The tenth platform houses an observatory with a capacity for 100 people. Its position, 560m above sea level, enables the visitor to enjoy a fine view of Barcelona and its surroundings. The observatory can be reached in less than two minutes via an external glass lift, travelling at the speed of 1m per second. In the reception area at the base of the tower you will find a cafeteria. The tower is linked to the Tibidabo Amusement Park (Tel. 211-7942) and the Tibidabo Funicular by internal transport which is free. The lift runs daily from 11am-7pm.

The Amusement Park of Tibidabo is hundreds of meters above sea level

The Museum of Science (Museu de la Ciència) is located at 55 Teodor Roviralta and is reached by buses nos. 17, 22, 58, 73, which are located nearby. It is open Tues.-Sun. from 10am-8pm, closed Monday. There is an entrance fee. Tel. 212-6050. In the museum is a planetarium and a wing devoted to the development of optics, mechanics, the study of sound waves, meteorology, computers, and other sciences.

The displays are intended to explain and simplify scientific and technological studies and processes. Various activities and programs on different subjects, especially for young people, are held here.

The **Clará Museum** is located at 27 Carrer Calatrava. You can reach it by taking the local train to Les Tres Torres station or any of the following buses: 14, 66, 70, 94 which bring you within walking distance of the museum. Open Tues.-Sun. from 9am-2pm, closed on Mondays, entrance free. Tel. 203-4058.

The house in which the museum is located was the home of one of Catalonia's foremost artists, Josep Clará 1878-1958). Along with his personal possessions and work tools, some of his sculptures, paintings, and sketches, are displayed covering all his years of artistic activity.

Enjoying the panoramic view of the city from the observatory of the Collserola Tower

Gaudí's Barcelona

Antoni Gaudí is, undoubtedly, one of the most well-known Catalonian personages throughout the world (except, perhaps, for the cellist, Pablo Casals). Gaudí was an architect and artist – one of the outstanding figures in modern architecture. His name is mentioned many times in the different tours of this guidebook, and indeed, this remarkable artist has placed his stamp on the city to such an extent that we have chosen to devote a special section to him and his works.

Antoni Gaudí was born in 1852 in the city of Reus, several dozens of kms from Barcelona. He completed his studies in Barcelona in 1878, and was active in the city during its days of glory and prosperity, so that he was afforded ample opportunities to exploit his talents.

At first, he was part of the modernistic trend, and was counted among a group of architects who changed the concept of design and construction in the city. Soon, however, at the end of the nineteenth century, he left the group, and his works began to deviate from historically accepted norms, as he formulated his own individualistic aesthetic principles. In most of his works he tried to depart from inflexibility in the use of construction materials. His buildings indeed excel in sculptural configurations "fluidity" of construction materials undulation of walls and unusual angles, and in the unconventional decorations and mosaics, while utilizing materials such as iron, stone, and ceramics. His style is unique, and he cannot be considered to belong to any particular trend. In 1926, Gaudí was tragically killed by the electric trolley of Barcelona.

Here is a description of a number of Gaudí's outstanding and important works in Barcelona, some of which have already been mentioned briefly in connection with different tour routes.

Sacred Family (Sagrada Familia) Church

The largest of Gaudí's works, considered to be one of the more famous symbols of Barcelona throughout the world, and one of the most compelling projects in the world of modernistic architecture. The Sacred Family Church remains unfinished to this day.

Gaudí began his work on this venturesome project in 1884, when he designed a structure which integrated different styles of construction – from the Gothic to his own ultramodern style. He wanted to design a "church for the twentieth century" by including in it all the architectonic knowledge which he had acquired. Here, Gaudí created a free, modern adaptation of the Gothic style.

A challenge to human imagination – the Sacred Family Church

The church design included three façades to symbolize the birth, suffering, and death of Jesus. On each façade, he planned four towers, each over 100 meters high: twelve towers in all, symbolizing the twelve disciples. One tower (170 meters high, and looking down on all the others) symbolizes Jesus; the four towers around him – the four Evangelists, and the last tower, rising over the apse, the Virgin Mother.

Gaudí's death in 1926 found the project still in its infancy, with only one façade, the "birth", and one tower completed. Work recommenced in 1940, but the fact that the artist failed to leave behind exact blueprints for completion of the project made the resumption of construction work more difficult. In any case, carrying out the project became a controversial matter, and it had to be financed by contributions. It is now estimated that the work will take another several dozens of years to complete.

In the small museum there is a model of the church, with graphic draughts of the different stages of its construction. In one of the underground rooms of the building, we find Gaudí's grave. The site is located at the corner of Mallorca and Sicilia Streets, and can be reached by taking the subway to the Sagrada Familia station (L5 line) or bus nos. 19, 20, 34, 43, 44, 45, 47, 50, 51 and 54.

Parc Güell

This unusual project is located at the northern end of the Gràcia Quarter. The park was commissioned and financed by the Barcelona financier Euseli Güell. He and his family are responsible for several of Gaudí's works in the city. The park was originally intended to be a neighborhood inhabited by sixty families, but the idea was never implemented and, in 1923 the park was transferred to the public domain. Only two houses were completed, and Gaudí himself bought one of them.

The Sacred Family Church – an integration of different building styles

Gaudí let his imagination run free in this project and the effect can be seen in unusual results. Near the entrance to the park are two houses, intended to be used for administra-

tion and gardening services for the neighborhood. Their unusual geometric forms, such as whimsical domes and walls covered with bits of ceramic and everyday items, are elements which repeat themselves. Especially impressive is the central square. Its borders are built in the form of a bench which is supported by 84 pillars in Doric style. Today Gaudí's house serves as a museum, displaying the possessions of this brilliant, nonconforming artist.

Unusual geometric forms at Parc Güell, situated at the northern end of the Gràcia quarter

The **Gaudí House-Museum** is open March-Nov. daily from 10am-2pm and 4-7pm, and is closed on Sat. Tel. 284-6446. The entrance to the park is on Olot Street, and you can reach it by taking the subway to the Lesseps station (L3 line) or buses 10, 24, 25 and 28.

Casa Milà (La Pedrera)

Casa Milà, also known as La Pedrera, dominates the corner of Passeig de Gràcia (no. 92) and Carrer Provença streets. This important modernistic work is an outstanding example of Gaudí's style.

The distinctive building serves to break the architectonic uniformity of the Eixample Quarter in which it is located. The wavy stone configurations are in stark contrast to the massive stone from which the building was constructed. The entrances to the building and the shops on its ground level resemble entrances to caves, and the round porches are finished with unique iron ornamentation.

Attic windows and chimneys of various shapes burst forth from the parabolic roof. You can visit the patios and the building's porch at set times (it is best to check with the tourist bureau).

It is possible to come by subway to either the Diagonal or the Passeig de Grácia station or by buses 16, 17, 22, 24, and 28. Tel. 487-3613. Guided tours of the house are conducted on Tues.-Sat., 10am, 11am, 12pm and 1pm. Tours last for 30 minutes and have commentaries in several languages.

Casa Batlló

Casa Batlló

Further along Passeig de Grà-cia, at no. 43, is another work of Gaudí. He renovated the building between 1904-1906 by request of one of Barcelona's wealthy citizens, Josep Batlló i Casanovas. Here, too, there is an interesting play on the combination of rigid materials, such as stone and iron, creating a variety of configurations of windows and porches, using a riot of colors. Pay special attention to the supporting pillars in the form of bones.

Those interested in visiting inside the building must get permission from the Gaudí Cathedra in the Barcelona Polytechnic (to reach the building, see directions for going to Casa Milà).

Casa Calvet

In the same area, at 48 Carrer Casp, between 1898-1900 Gaudí built a building which won him a special prize from the Barcelona municipality. The work was commissioned by the Calvet family, a family of textile manufacturers. The house is still used as a private residence.

The façade of the building, decorated with sculptures, and the entrance hall were inspired by the baroque style, whereas the inner rooms and porches excel in their functionalism. The furniture of the apartment on the first floor was designed by Gaudí, and some of it has been preserved in the Gaudí Museum in Güell Park.

Casa Calvet – Gaudí won a special prize from the Barcelona municipality for this work

The nearest subway station is Urquinaoana (lines L1 and L4); or take buses 45 and 47.

Güell Palace
(Palau Güell)

This work of Gaudí was commissioned by the Güell family and executed between 1886-1888. Here, Gaudí first applied his innovative ideas and his interpretation of the old styles. The construction is influenced by the Gothic style and by Moslem ornamental elements.

The basement floor, intended for stables, is built of small arches, held up by wide supporting pillars. The ground floor was meant for administrative use. In the center of the first floor, the floor used by the nobility, is the main salon, where lectures, meetings and concerts were held, and encircling the

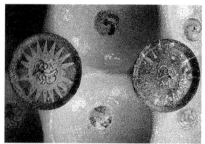

salon, are the various family rooms. The interior design was inspired by the most outstanding features that characterized the period – marble pillars, imposing arches and ceillings of the finest wood.

The building is located at 3 Nou de Rambla, and today it houses the Theater Insitute of Barcelona (see "The Rambla"), which is open to the public from 10am-1pm and 5-7pm. Guided tours daily at 10am, 11am, 12pm and 1pm. Tel. 317-3974.

Pavellons Güell

Built between 1884-1887 and commissioned by the Güell family, the structure was intended for the use of the gateman of the Pedralbes Palace – which then belonged to the wealthy Güell family – and was also meant to serve as the palace stables. Today, it houses the Gaudí cathedra of the College of Architecture of the Barcelona Polytechnic (see "Pedralbes" route).

The huge pillars which support Parc Güell's central square

Casa Vicens

This luxurious villa was built by Gaudí for the ceramics industrialist Manuel Vicens i Mantaner. As it is one of the artist's first works, the straight line is still dominant. But Gaudí let his imagination express itself in copious decorations, designed under Moslem influence. Today it is a private home. The address: no. 22 Les Carolines, the nearest subway stations are Lesseps (L3 line) and Gràcia; and the buses which bring you here are nos. 22, 24, 25, 31 and 32. The towers of the sacred Family Church.

The towers of the Sacred Family Church

EXCURSIONS

In the following pages, we have added a few suggested tours, beyond Catalonia's capital, Barcelona. Included here are the highlights of the region, such as the village of Sitges, the coastline of Costa Brava, and the Montserrat Monastery. These excursions are either a day tour or part of a longer exploration of the region and are highly recommended.

Beaches

THE MUNICIPAL BEACH

This beach is not well liked by the locals because of its proximity to the port and the industrial areas, even though the beach itself is quite clean and pleasant. To reach it, take the subway to the Ciutadella station (line L4), and continue on foot. If you have more time at your disposal, there are much nicer beaches you can visit in the vicinity.

Beaches to the south of the city

Castelldefels: A nearby beach, only a fifteen minute ride from the city, but less exciting than the Sitges beach. Bathing in the nude is permitted at the Torro Bravo

campsite attached to this beach. To reach it, take the UC bus which leaves from Plaça Universitat.

The beach at Sitges

Sitges: A marvelous beach town, forty minutes away by train from the Sants station. In addition to the beach, there are a restaurant, bars, and other attractions. In a part of this beach, fully nude bathing is permitted. (See also the entry on the town of Sitges in this section below.)

Beaches to the north of the city

Vilasar de Mar: This is rather a mediocre beach, located about 40 minutes away from Barcelona. To reach the better beaches, it is necessary to go past Mataró.

Sant Pol de Mar: A good beach about an hour away from the city. During the summer, it may be quite crowded, in which case it is worth going a little further north.

Calella: This beach, located about 15 minutes north of Sant Pol de Mar, is considered to be the best in the area. In many parts of it, nude bathing is permitted. Very worthwhile to visit.

Important for those going to the northern beaches: during the summer season the beaches are crowded. There are also long lines at the ticket booths for the train at the Sants station (sometimes there is up to an hour wait), so it is worth catching the train going north at either the Passeig de Gràcia or the Plaça de Catalunya station (*Renfe* train).

Sitges

About 37 kms south of Barcelona is the town of Sitges. This friendly town of 10,000 inhabitants boasts about 5 kms of bathing beaches. Because of them, it has become a popular vacation site. The church which overlooks the beach was built between the sixteenth and eighteenth centuries. The illu-

CATALONIA

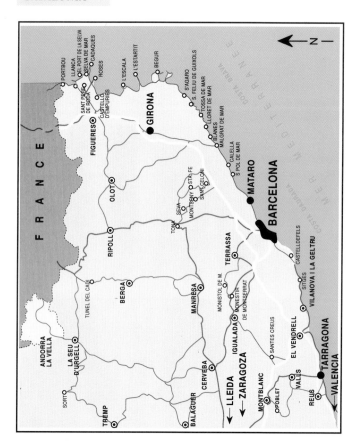

mination around it at night is very impressive. Next to the church is the home of the painter Santiago Rusiñol, who settled here at the end of the last century. Using stones taken from the ruins of an ancient fortress

At Sitges, a lovely beach town not far from Barcelona

which stood here, Rusiñol built his home on the foundations of the homes of fishermen. Today, the house serves as a museum, Museu Cau Ferrat. A visit here is very worthwhile both for the impressive building and for the collection of paintings in it (including works by El Greco and Rusiñol himself). It is open Tues.-Sun. from 10am-1:30pm and 4-6pm. For more information call the Sitges Municipal Tourist Office at the "Oasis" Bus Terminal, Tel. 811-7630.

Another museum in this town is Casa Llopis. This house was built at the end of the eighteenth century and, today, it houses a collection of the family possessions of the wealthy of that period (open during the same hours as the previously mentioned museum). (Your entrance ticket is also valid for Casa Papinol in Vilanova i la Geltrú.)

It is easy to reach Sitges from the Sants train station in Barcelona. Trains for Sitges, run frequently all day.

During the local Corpus Cristi celebrations which take place in the spring, for one or two days, the entire town becomes a huge carpet of flowers.

VILANOVA I LA GELTRÚ

Located a few kms past Sitges, the town has 40,000 inhabitants. It, too, has a popular beach, but it isn't as long as that of Sitges.

Tarragona

At Sitges, the home of the painter Rusiñol, built of stones taken from the ruins of an ancient fortress

About 100 kms from Barcelona, on the main road to Valencia, we find the city of Tarragona with its 120,000 inhabitants. Tarraconesis, as it was called by the Romans, was their large and powerful stronghold in the Iberian Peninsula, and one of their important ports, starting from the third century BC. Today, it is a lively, modern city, which makes every effort to preserve the remains of its glorious past. (You can take either the *Renfe* train from the Barcelona Sant Central and Passeig de Gràcia stations, or the *Hispania Reus* bus line from the corner of P. de San Joan and Disputació streets, Tel. (977) 30-1134. The local tourist office is located at 46 Rambla Nova, Tel. (977) 23-2143.

We begin our tour of the city from the main street, Rambla Nova, which is somewhat reminiscent of the Rambla in Barcelona. Here, too, there is a broad boulevard with much green in the middle. At the end of the boulevard is the Balcó del Mediterani (Mediterranean balcony), overlooking the sea, with a Roman amphitheater down below.

From the balcony, we go northwest on Rambla Nova to Sant Francesc Street, where we turn right to Rambla Vella. On Rambla

A relaxed atmosphere at a Spanish town

Vella we turn left to Via de l'Imperi. This route will take us to one of the most impressive ruins from the Roman period, the **Passeig Arqueológic** (the Archeological promenade) which extends along the impressive walls of the ancient city (open every day from 9am-7pm). We continue with the Promenade as far as St. Anthony's Gateway (Portal de Sant Antoni), through which we can enter the old city. Here, we turn left on Granada Street to the **Archeological Museum** (Museu Arqueológic). It is open Tues.-Sat. from 10am-1pm and 4:30-8pm (in winter until 7pm), on Sun. 10am-2pm, closed Mondays and holidays. This interesting museum displays a selection of archeological finds from Tarragona and the environs, mostly from the Roman period – tools, coins, mosaics, and statues.

As we leave the museum and head toward Plaça del Rei, we turn into one of the streets which lead to Carrer Major. On this street we turn left to the **cathedral**, which suddenly comes into view at the end of the street, at Plaça de la Seu. Its construction

was begun in the twelfth century, and one of the windows on its façade, the huge "rose" is particularly impressive. Inside the cathedral are many chapels. An ornate altar in the center of the apse is dedicated to the patron saint of the city, Saint Thecla.

Other Roman ruins: at the southern end of the city in Avinguda Ramón i Cayal, are the remains of a cemetery of the first Christians in Tarragona – **Necrópoli Paleocristi** (open during the same hours as the Archeological Museum). This "city of the dead" has been preserved as it was, and you can observe, scattered about, hundreds of graves. Some of the most interesting sarcophagi which were found here are on display in the museum.

Poblet

Located forty-five kms northwest of Tarragona, about 140 kms from Barcelona, is one of the more beautiful Spanish monasteries. The **Poblet Monastery**, Tel. (977) 870-254, was founded in the twelfth century by Ramón Berenguer IV, who wanted to show his appreciation to God for His help in defeating the Moors and returning Spain to Christian hands (the Reconquista).

As time passed, the monastery gained eminence and became an important religious center. It was even chosen to be the pantheon of the kings of Aragón and Catalonia. But the Napoleonic Wars and the decline in stature of religion caused the flourishing monastery to sink into oblivion. Today, some monks still maintain the community there. It is a rare specimen of medieval and Gothic architecture at its most beautiful.

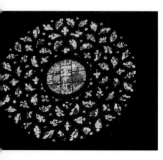

At the monastery church, note the magnificent altar from the sixteenth century. It is also possible to visit the pantheon which has undergone large-scale reconstruction. The big churchyard is especially impressive and is a clear indication of the importance of the place in times past.

If you come by car from Barcelona, leave the city going south on the express highway to Valencia. Then, turn off on road A2 in the direction of Saragossa. It is also possible to go by train from Barcelona to Tarragona. From there, buses leave for Lleida which pass by the monastery.

Santes Creus Monastery

About 40 kms before Poblet, on road A2, if you are travelling by car, you will pass another monastery from the same period, **Santes Creus**, Tel. (977) 638-329. Unlike the Poblet Monastery, this one is no longer in use, and serves only as a museum.

The Santes Creus Monastery was founded only a few years after the establishment of the Poblet Monastery, and it, too, had its days of grandeur – until the Napoleonic army reached the area.

Shaded, narrow alleys are a common sight in Spain

Between the two monasteries is the town of **Montblanc**, which, today, has 5,000 inhabitants. Its story is similar to that of the other monasteries – it, too, was founded in the twelfth century. And it, too, enjoyed the favor of the crown of Aragón and Catalonia, as witnessed by the remains of the wall of the city and a number of Gothic buildings, including that which houses the local museum. The Santa Maria church, which towers over the town, was built in the fourteenth century but was never completed.

Montserrat

In the heart of the majestic and unique Montserrat mountain range lies an important Benedictine monastery, the **Monastery of Montserrat**. It was founded in the eleventh century as a small, humble house of prayer.

The majestic Montserrat Mountain range

With the addition of more monks, the building was expanded from time to time, so that, eventually, there was a jumble of building styles. In 1812, the monastery was plundered and almost destroyed by Napoleon's army. The present building was reconstructed and renovated in the nineteenth century. Its importance to the Christian world and its marvelous location, about 1,000 meters above the valley of the Llobregat River, among the towering cliffs, made the site a magnet for both tourists and pilgrims.

The monastery itself is closed to visitors, but you can visit the monastery church, where you can see a statue of the "Black Madonna", a wooden statue from the twelfth century. It is displayed inside a glass cabinet above the upper altar, and there is usually a long line waiting to see it. There is also a famous boys' choir (Escolanía), founded in the twelfth century, which sings in the church. Next to the church is the museum of the monastery, which exhibits, among other things, works by El Greco and Caravaggio.

From the monastery, you can go for a walk among the rocks, where there are many niches and small chapels. Also, two cable-cars climb upward, from the monastery, one to the San Joan Hermitage Chapel and the other to Santa Cova. According to tradition, the statue of the "Black Madonna" was discovered at Santa Cova. The walk from the cablecar station at the top to either site takes about half an hour.

There is also a path from the monastery which leads to San Miguel (about half an hour's walk), where there is a fine view of the monastery.

Another walk is up to the Sant Jeroni summit, at a height of 1238 meters above sea level. The road which goes from the Montserrat Monastery to the Santa Cecilia Church will bring you to the ascending cablecar which takes you most of the way up to the summit. There, on a clear day, you can see a panoramic view from the Pyrenee Mountains to the seashore. From the summit, it is possible to continue on a path offering wonderful views and reach San Joan, next to the Montserrat monastery.

You can also reach Montserrat from Barcelona by car on the road to Lleida and, from there, turn off at the village of Monistrol. There, you will find a winding road, which continues for about 20 kms, and leads to the monastery (about 60 kms in all). An alternative would be to take the train from Barcelona (from Plaça d'Espanya) to the lower station of the funicular which climbs up to the monastery.

Montseny

If you have not yet had your fill of mountains and marvelous landscapes, and have the use of a car, it would be worth your while to take a trip of several hours from Barcelona to the Montseny Mountain Range, one of the more impressive branches of the Pyrenees. The highest peaks of this range reach a height of over 1,700 meters above sea level.

A number of routes cut through these granite hills, affording magnificent views. Those leaving Barcelona on the expressway going north should turn left to Sant Celoni, the town at the foot of these hills, to the east. From here, a marvelous road, 20 kms long, climbs up to Santa Fe in the heart of the mountains.

After returning to Sant Celoni, there are two alternatives for continuing to tour the range

– from the north or from the south. From the northern road, a road leads to East Hilari Sacalm, a charming vacation resort village in a wonderful location. The southern route is the shorter of the two.

It is possible to go around the mountain from the north or the south and return to Sant Celoni and the express highway, but it is also possible to choose one or the other of these roads and go on to Tona near the western base of the mountain. From there, the road turns south to Barcelona.

Girona

This "city of a thousand conquests" got its name because of its strategic location on the main route between the French border and Barcelona, at the confluence of the Ter and Onyar Rivers. Its walls were rebuilt again and again throughout its history – from the period of the Iberians until the days of Napoleon, who required many months to complete his conquest.

Today the city numbers about 75,000 inhabitants. The lanes of its old city are especially interesting. It is worth the time to stroll around them with no special aim in mind. The Carrer Força in the center of the old city was the main street of the Jewish quarter, which flourished here during the thirteenth century. It leads to the local **cathedral**, which is reached by climbing tens

The tower of Sant Felíu Church in Girona, housing several sarcophagi

of steps. The façade of the structure is baroque, and the rest Gothic.

In addition to seeing the chapels of the cathedral and noting the beautiful altar, a visit should be made to the rooms which house its treasures. Here, there are gold and silver objects, Bibles – the earliest from the tenth century, and a huge wall hanging, depicting Jesus and the Creation. Returning on Carrer Força, we pass the arch which used to be part of the fortress which defended the city walls and arrive at Sant Felíu Church, where there are several fine sarcophagi. Nearby are the **Arab Baths** (Banyos Arabs) from the thirteenth century, which resemble in style baths in other Moslem cities.

The local tourist bureau, at 1 Rambla de la Llibertat, is open Mon.-Fri. from 8am-8pm, on Sat. from 8am-2pm and 4-8pm, closed on Sundays. Tel. (972) 419-419. You can reach the city by car on the expressway which goes from Barcelona to the French border (it takes about an hour), by the *Renfe* train from the Barcelona Sants Central and Passeig de Gràcia Stations, or by the *Barcelona Bus* line from the Estació d'Autobusos Barcelona Nord.

Costa Brava

Northeast of Barcelona is one of Spain's more beautiful and popular beach areas – a coastline stretching for hundreds of kilometers, with inlets, cliffs, palm trees, bathing beaches, resort towns, and lots of sunshine. Until not so long ago, Costa Brava, with its small fishing villages, was largely unknown. But now, since its discovery by tourists and thanks to the growing awareness by the locals of its tourist potential for this part of the country, the area has become a major tourist attraction. Picturesque villages and towns, with numerous hotels and tourist services were developed and have become popular vacations sites. The Costa Brava tourist office is in Girona, Tel.(972) 208-401.

Those who want to vacate in one of the resorts along the shores of the Costa Brava would do well to reserve accommodations in advance during the summer. You can reach the beaches by the *Sarfa* bus line from the Estació d'Autobusos Barcelona Nord, Tel. 265-1158. Those simply interested in getting to know the region can make do with a one or two day trip from Barcelona, and stop, at will, to enjoy a beach or a town en route. About 70 kms northeast of Barcelona is the town of **Blanes**, with its 20,000 inhabitants. The Costa Brava stretches north from here to Port Bou on the French border (150 kms away). The tourist boom which has hit this entire area, causing unlimited development, has also affected Blanes.

Blanes boasts a quiet, protected harbor and a small fishing port. The botanical gardens are worth visiting, not only because of the wide array of plants displayed but also because of the lovely views from here out to sea.

Twenty kms from Blanes we arrive at the town of **Tossa de Mar**, one of the first tourist sites along the Costa Brava. The old section of the town, Vila Vella, is especially suited for a leisurely walk, and you will enjoy going up to the beautiful Gothic church, with its views of the Tossa harbor area.

Twenty-five kms separate Tossa de Mar from the next seaside town, **Sant Felíu de Guíxols**. Attention should be paid to this marvelous stretch of shoreline – the road winds between tiny bays and small inlets.

Sant Felíu itself has no bathing beaches, but it offers relatively cheap accommodations and charming restaurants and bars. Only a few kilometers from here is **S'Agaró** which has pleasant and enjoyable bathing beaches but expensive tourist services.

From here until Begur, the coastline has the same kind of rugged rocky terrain. A large number of vacation sites are located in this area.

L'Estratit is a picturesque resort town with several kilometers of lovely coastline. Opposite it, a number of islands rise out of the sea. North of the town are the ruins of the ancient city of **Empúries**. In the sixth century BC, the Greek polis of Emporion was founded here. The city flourished and grew in importance with the arrival of Julius Caesar, in the middle of the first century BC. It continued to prosper until the third century AD, after which it began to suffer from recurring invasions, until it was destroyed in the eighth century by the Moors. The remains are not very impressive – a number of columns and painted walls and floors which were restored.

White sands, the sea breeze and tasty Spanish food

Here the scenery changes, and the two rivers, Fluviá and Ter, make it appear more gentle and green. But, beginning at the town of **Roses**, you, again, encounter cliffs that drop precariously into the sea. This resort town is located on the remains of an ancient Greek city. Its harbor is revealed in all its glory from Super Roses Hill.

Among the resort villages found north of

Flying kites on the beach is a pleasant pastime

here, it is worth noting **Cadaqués** which is in the center of Cape Creus, In the eighteenth and nineteenth centuries it was a flourishing fishing town, and recently it has become a tourist center – without losing its special character. Among the artists who made their home here was Salvador Dali.

If we have already come this far, we should not miss **Sant Pere de Roda**, the remains of a Benedictine monastery from the tenth century. Although it has been deserted since the eighteenth century, the building is still well preserved, with its two bell towers. It is located almost at the summit of the mountain in the center of Cape Creus (about 600 meters above sea level), and the view from here is breathtaking. You can reach the monastery by climbing up on foot (about an hour) from the town of Port de la Selva or by car on a road which passes near the monastery (leaving another 15 minute climb on foot).

Andorra

More than 200 kms north of Barcelona is the autonomous principality of Andorra with its unusual history. This small principality, whose entire area covers 460 sq/km numbers 30,000 inhabitants, who are proud of their independent past. They have almost no contact with their neighbors. The tourist office is located at 159 Mariá Cubí, Tel. 200-0787.

An exquisitely decorated drinking fountain

Since the thirteenth century, two princes have divided the government of Andorra between them – the Bishop of Seu d'Urgell (the Spanish city near Andorra just before the border crossing) and the French Duke of Foix. Together, the two neighbor princes delineated the spheres of government, and feudal law has preserved the dual government for their descendants – the bishop and the French president (to whom the authority of the Duke of Foix was transferred).

Actually, until the beginning of this century, Andorra was almost completely isolated from its neighbors, mainly because it was set in the heart of the Pyrenees and its wild mountain terrain made access to it and through it difficult. Only at the beginning of the century was a road paved, connecting Andorra with Spain. In the 1930's, the road connecting it with France was paved (even now, the road to France is blocked by snow during the winter months). This connection linking it to the outer world greatly changed the way of life here – from an agricultural district whose main source of income was cattle raising, the principality quickly became a center of smuggling. Today, thanks to the fact that no taxes or customs are collected here, most of its income comes from tourists who arrive in droves to purchase items cheaply. The height of the Pyrenees Mountains in Andorra is over 2500 meters above sea level. It also has two large valleys, Valira del Nord (the "northern valley") and Valira del Oriente (the "eastern valley"). The two rivers which form the valleys join in a single river which flows south, becoming one of the sources of the Ebro River and forming the Gran Valira (the "Grand Valley") Transportation by *Alsina Graells* bus line from 4 Rda. Universitat, Tel. 265-6508. There are also one-day and two-day tours, organized by *Julia Tours* (Tel. 317-6454) and *Pullmantur* (Tel. 317-1297).

Andorra la Vella, the capital of Andorra, is located near the confluence of the two rivers. The town, which numbers 10,000 inhabitants, has become a shopping center, attracting droves of tourists during the summer. During that season, the roads are jammed. So, you should try and park your car on the outskirts of town.

The only building worth visiting here is the Casa de la Vall. It houses the Andorra parliament and its court of justice. This massive structure is open to the public Mon.-Fri. from 9-10am and 3-4pm, on Sat., only in the morning; on Sundays and when it is in session, it is closed to the public. The outskirts of the city adjoin the neighboring town of Les Escaldes, a popular spa.

Those wanting to enjoy nature more than to shop in Andorra can leave the capital via either of two roads: one which leads north along the Valira del Nord (10 kms) or another which leads northeast along the Valira del Oriente (3 kms). The latter goes to the highest mountain pass in the Pyrenees, **Envalira Pass**, 2400 meters above sea level. From here, the road winds downward sharply to the French border crossing.

Travelers to Andorra should take into consideration that for all intents and purposes they will be crossing a border. They will need a passport and should make sure that their Spanish visa allows them to re-enter the country. Both the Spanish peseta and the French franc are equally acceptable in Andorra. The only official language is Catalan but, of course, Spanish and French are also spoken. (the English language is usually of no use).

A typical house in Andorra, an autonomous principality situated over 200 kilometers north of Barcelona

"MUSTS"

Some of European culture's most beautiful objects are concentrated in Barcelona, especially in the fields of architecture and painting. In the following pages we will indicate some of the sites which make the city unique, and should not be missed during your visit to Catalonia's capital.

The Gothic Quarter – the wonderful quarter which began to develop during the Roman period. It includes towering cathedrals, beautiful palaces, and interesting lanes. It is best to enter the quarter from Plaça Nova and stroll around, going back in time to the world of the city's rulers during the stormy Middle Ages (see "The Gothic Quarter").

The Cathedral – the cathedral of Barcelona, the old city's heart of hearts. A visit here gives an appreciation of the wealth and power of the city and of the centrality of religion in the life of the community. Also, not to be missed is the garden of the cathedral which is nearby (see "The Gothic Quarter").

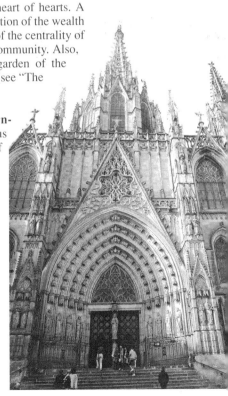

The Catalonian Government Palace – a glorious palace and a source of pride for the local population, since it is the symbol of Catalonian power. Enter from Plaça Sant Jaume, but make arrangements to do so in advance (see "The Gothic Quarter").

Sagrada Familia Church – the ultimate creation among the works of the architectural genius Gaudí. A challenge to human imagination and perception of space and distance. The church is in the eastern part of the city, and it is easiest to reach via subway line L5 (blue) to the station bearing the name of the church. Don't miss a visit to this church and the climb to the top of the building either on foot or by elevator (see "Gaudí's Barcelona").

Plaça Reial, a pleasant and tranquil spot in the heart of the vibrant city

Santa Maria del Mar Church – the oldest, most beautiful church in the city. Marvelous, airy architecture; Gothic style at its best. Not far from the Picasso Museum (see "From the Picasso Museum to the Zoo").

Picasso Museum – richly endowed and impressive. The visitor follows the evolution of the artist's genius. The museum is located in a beautiful palace of the aristocracy from the fourteenth century at nos. 14-19 Montcada Street. This should not be missed even by those who are not avid art enthusiasts (see "From the Picasso Museum to the Zoo").

Güell Park – another site of the genius, Gaudí. In this park the famous architect combines his architectonic principles with the landscape, and the result is astonishing. Not to be missed (especially with children) (see "Gaudí's Barcelona").

The Spanish Village (Poble Espanyol) – located on top of Montjuïc, built for the 1929 exhibition. Today, you can visit the buildings of the "village", representing different cities and regions in Spain. A commercialized tourist center, not lacking a certain Spanish charm (see "Montjuïc").

Miró Foundation – This museum contains many marvelous works of the well-known painter and sculptor. It is located in an impressive modernistic building, especially designed by a friend of the artist. Obligatory for art and painting enthusiasts (see "Montjuïc").

The Ramblas – the vibrant artery of the city. There are a variety of small and large shops, cafés and restaurants, as well as street musicians on this shady boulevard. Best to avoid the lower section of the boulevard after dark (see "The Ramblas").

Tibidabo

The La Boqueria Market – a popular fruit, vegetable, fish, etc. market in the center of the city. Happy, informal atmosphere. Easy to reach from the Ramblas Boulevard. It's fitting to end your tour with a tasty meal in one of the small restaurants in the lanes surrounding the market (see "The Ramblas").

The central square of Güell Park is supported by eighty-four pillars in Doric style

Tibidabo – amusement park and marvelous observation point, overlooking Barcelona from the heights of the northwestern part of the city. Scenery and entertainment. The recommended way to climb up to Tibidabo is via the

Have yourself portrayed by a Rambla artist

"Blue Tram" which leaves Pla. John F. Kennedy and then continue by *funicular* to the top of the hill (see "Tibidabo").

MAKING THE MOST OF YOUR STAY

The Catalonian cuisine

The Catalonian cuisine resembles the Spanish cuisine, with a number of special gastronomic variants. Here, the emphasis is on vegetables, fish, and seafood. The Barcelonian cuisine includes a wide gamut of dishes unique to the area, and many courses in large meals. Breakfast is usually continental, and includes coffee and a pastry (usually a croissant). Black coffee is *café solo*, and coffee with milk is *café con leche*.

The Spanish are great lovers of good food and devote much attention to it. The two main meals are lunch – usually served between 2-3:30pm, always a hot meal with a number of dishes, served with wine; and supper – served late, around 9pm. Supper is either a smaller version of lunch or else it is a meal made up of different soups, salads, cheeses and sausages. On weekends, and especially on Sundays, it is the practice in Barcelona to eat lunch later than on other days of the week, that is, at around 4pm, and to eat less in the evening.

Try to be receptive to unfamiliar food from the Barcelona cuisine, and dare to taste specialities of the Catalonian cuisine.

Among the dishes which are especially popular in the area are many tasty seafoods, with the emphasis on snails, which are much loved by Barcelonians.

Here is a short list of recommended local dishes:

Paella – a bowl of rice and seafood. The Paella is well-known in all of Spain, and especially in Catalonia. It is a marvelous dish, made of tomatoes and seafood, cooked together: it originated in the Zarzuela region.

The Paella, a dish made of rice and seafood, is very popular in Barcelona

Paella amb tomagueti perniz – bread with mashed tomato and cheese on it (served as either an appetizer or a side dish along with the main course).

179

Faves a la Catalana – beans baked with vegetables.

Butifarra amb mongetes – white beans with pork sausage (appetizer).

Habas catalans – beans (lime) with pork (appetizer).

Carn d'Olla – meat soup with many kinds of meat (during the winter).

Escudella – the same soup but without the meat (unique to this area).

Bolets, Bovenons – wild mushrooms, unique to this area, during the autumn.

Canalons – like Italian canneloni, more popular in Catalonia than in other parts of Spain.

Tapas – a platter with a selection of the restaurant's dishes. It makes for a satisfying meal.

Revellons – excellent dish made of mushrooms, seasoned according to the best local gastronomic tradition.

Jortell, Coca de sant Joan – thick pastry with sugared nuts and fruits, for dessert.

Jerez wine – excellent sparkling wine, a recommended addition to the Catalonian dishes. It is the practice to order it in restaurants where these dishes are served.

The menu

A typical meal will start with soups (*sopes*), followed by appetizers (*entrans*). After the appetizers, come eggs (*ous*), fish (*peix*) and meat (*carnes*). The various kinds of meat offerred usually include chicken (*pol-lastre*), beef (*bov*), and pork (*porc*) or shellfish (*marisc*). Most are: fried (*fregid*), in a batter of eggs and flour (*romana*), or grilled (*a la plancha*). After the main course, comes the dessert (*postre*). Popular desserts include: *flan* or fruits in season (*fruitas del temps*).

Along with the regular menu, there is also the "special of the day" (*menu del dia*), which includes a list of appetizers (A) and main courses (B). The customer must choose one dish from group A and one from group B, along with bread (*pan*), wine (*vino*), and a dessert of his/her choice, for a set price. This meal is much cheaper than putting together the same meal from the regular menu, and it offers a choice. This custom originated in the law which controlled the prices of meals, taking into consideration the limited means of

poverty-stricken workers and, today, it has become the practice in most restaurants, except for the most exclusive.

Restaurants

Gastronomically, Barcelona is the meeting point for the different types of Spanish cuisine. This means that, in addition to the unique Catalonian dishes, you can find many restaurants in the city that specialize in dishes which are representative of the culinary tradition of various regions in Spain (Basque, Galician, Valencian, Castillian).

Along with the varied Spanish food, in Barcelona it is

possible to find restaurants which specialize in the preparation of food from other countries, as you will see below. Even the American hamburger has its place here.

Barcelona boasts many good restaurants, some in the famous quarters of the city, and some on the seashore, as befits a port city.

Many restaurants are closed on Saturday nights and Sundays, and some close for vacation during the month of August; so you should check before planning your next meal. In the most exclusive restaurants, it is advisable to reserve in advance.

This chapter recommends a wide variety of restaurants, located in different parts of the city. The categories relate to the type of foods served and the cost of the meal. The prices charged are

noted according to the following key:

Very expensive – over $75 per meal.
Expensive – between $45-$75.
Moderate – between $20-$45.
Inexpensive – less than $20.

CATALONIAN CUISINE

Orotava: 335 Consell de Cent, Tel. 487-7374. Closed Sunday. Specializes in typical Catalonian and northern Spanish foods. Excellent game dishes. Reserve in advance (very expensive).

Reno: 27 Tuset, Tel. 200-5129. Open all year. Elegant restaurant, specializing in excellent Catalonian foods, also offers French dishes. Reserve in advance (very expensive).

Agut d'Avignon: 3 Trinidad, Tel. 302-6034. Closed Sunday and during Easter week.

Rural atmosphere, but not rural prices. Recommended. Reserve in advance (expensive).

La Cuineta: 4 Paradis, Tel. 315-0111. Closed Monday. Intimate and pleasant, located in an old building from the seventeenth century. Known for its good service (expensive).

Passadis dén Pep: 2 Pla. de Palau, Tel. 301-1021. Closed Mondays, holidays, and during the month of August. Reserve in advance (expensive).

Parellada Garrell, R: 37 Argentera, Tel. 315-4010. Closed Sunday. Very "in" during recent years (not expensive).

Agut: 16 Gignàs, Tel. 315-1709. Closed Sunday afternoon, Monday, and during the month of July. Simple and good (moderate).

Egipto: 12 Jerusalem, Tel. 317-7480. Small and excellent, serves fine home-cooking. Located near the Boqueria market (moderate).

Chicoa: 73 Aribau, Tel. 453-1123. Closed Saturdays, Sundays, holidays, and during the month of August. Good restaurant, pleasantly designed (moderate).

El Turia: 7 Ca. de Petxina, the entrance to the lane is from 85 Ramblas. Tel. 317-9507. Closed Sunday. Small restaurant, located behind the market. Serves tasty, fresh food (inexpensive).

BASQUE CUISINE
Beltxenea: 275 Mallorca, Tel. 215-3024. Closed Saturday afternoon and Sunday. Considered one of the best restaurants which serve Basque food (very expensive).

Guria: 97 Casanova, Tel. 253-6325. Open all year (very expensive).

Amaya: 20 Rambla Sta. Monica, Tel. 302-1037. Open all year (expensive).

GALICIAN CUISINE
Botafumeiro: 81 Gran de Gràcia, Tel. 218-4230. Closed Sunday nights, Mondays, and during the month of August (very expensive).

Casa Duro: 271 Provença, Tel. 215-3237. Open all year. Serves the best Galician dishes. Recommended to order fish (expensive).

Medulio: 6 Av. Princep d'Astúries, Tel. 217-3868. Closed Sunday evenings (moderate).

VALENCIAN CUISINE
Aguír: 8 Riereta, Tel. 329-9555. Closed Sunday and Monday afternoons, and during the month of August (moderate).

CASTILIAN CUISINE
El Asador de Aranda: 31 Av. Tibidabo, Tel. 417-0115. Closed Sunday nights (very expensive).

INTERNATIONAL CUISINE

El Dorada Petit: 51 Dolors Monserdá, Tel. 204-5153. Closed Sundays and for two weeks during August. Located in a private villa, and considered one of the best in Barcelona. Superior cuisine! (very expensive).

Vía Veneto: 10 Gandúxer, Tel. 200-7244. Highly recommended both for the excellent cuisine and for its good service (very expensive).

Finisterre: 469 Av. Diagonal, Tel. 439-5576. Closed during the month of August. Excellent food. Reservation must be made in advance (very expensive).

Flash Flash Tortilleria: 25 La Granada del Penedés, Tel. 237-0990. Open until 1:30am. Serves a unique and varied selection of omlettes. Recommended! (moderate).

Giardinetto Notte: 22 La Granada del Penedés, Tel. 218-7536. Closed Sundays and during the month of August (moderate).

FISH AND SEAFOOD

Along the Barcelona seashore you can find a large concentration of restaurants specializing in seafood. These restaurants are also found in other parts of the city. We have selected some of the best and recommend them to you:

La Dorada: 44-46 Trav. Gràcia, Tel. 200-6322. Closed Sunday. A paradise for lovers of fish and seafood. Reserve in advance (very expensive).

La Cúpula: 37 Teodoro Roviralta, Tel. 212-4888. Open all year (expensive).

La Mercantil Peixatera: 117 Aribau, Tel. 253-3599. Closed on Monday afternoons (expensive).

Set Portes: 14 P. Isabel II, Tel. 319-3033. Closed on holidays

A fascinating mixture of colors, sounds and aromas at the Boqueria Market

and during the month of August. Good fish restaurant, located in a lovely building of modern design. Reserve in advance (expensive).

Casa Leopoldo: 24 Sant Rafael, Tel. 441-3041. Closed on Sunday evenings, Mondays, during Easter week, and during the month of August (moderate).

Can Solé: 4 Sant Carlos, Tel. 319-5012. Closed on Saturday night and all day Sunday. Closed the first two weeks of February and the first two weeks of September. Wide variety of seafoods (moderate).

Los Caracoles: 14 Escudellers, Tel. 301-2041. Specializes in preparing snails and is very well known for its atmosphere and the quality of its food (moderate).

Can Tipa: 6 Pl. Nacional, Tel. 319-7032. Closed on Tuesdays and during the month of November. Romantic beach restaurant (moderate).

FRENCH CUISINE

Neichel: 16 Av. Pedralbes, Tel. 203-8408. Closed Sundays, holidays, and during the month of August. This is one of the best restaurants in all of Spain (very expensive).

Vinya-Rosa: 17 Av. Sarriá, Tel. 430-0003. Closed Sundays (expensive).

El Gran Café: 9 Avinyó, Tel. 318-7986. Closed Sundays. Lovely restaurant, decorated in the style of the beginning of the century. French and local cuisine (expensive).

Casa Quirze: 202 Laureano Miró, Tel. 371-1084. Closed

Sunday nights, Mondays, and during the week of Easter. Outstanding (moderate).

Hostal Sant Jordi: 123 Traverssera de Dalt, Tel. 213-1037. Closed Sunday evenings and during the month of August. Specializes in French dishes and also Catalonian food. Highly recommended. Though not expensive, it is of a high standard (moderate).

La Venta: Pl. Doctor Andreu, Tel. 212-6455. Closed Sundays. For lovers of the "nouvelle cuisine". It is best to come at night, sit outside and enjoy the view. Reserve in advance (expensive).

ITALIAN CUISINE

Tramonti 1980: 501 Av. Diagonal, Tel. 410-1535. Outstanding restaurant, located next to the Plaça Francesc Mari (moderate).

La Borda: 42 Passeig Manuel Girona, Tel. 204-5118. Closed on Monday nights (moderate).

Robot Jordi: 45 Bori i

Fontestá, Tel. 201-2577. Open all year (inexpensive).

INDONESIAN FOOD

Bali: Parc d'Atraccions, Montjuïc, Tel. 441-3084. Located on the tourist route, first-rate Indonesian food. Suitable for large groups but not for an intimate meal (expensive).

JAPANESE FOOD

Kiyokata: 231 Muntaner, Tel. 200-5126. Closed Mondays. Best to reserve place in advance (moderate).

GRILL

La Senyora Grill: 45 Bori i Fontestá, Tel. 201-2577. Open all year (expensive).

A La Menta: 50 Passeig Manuel Girona, Tel. 204-1549. Closed Sunday evenings, also closed Saturdays during the month of August. Best to reserve a table in advance. The meat is superior (moderate).

VEGETARIAN FOOD

Self Naturista: 15 Santa Anna, Tel. 302-2130. Closed Sundays and holidays. Self-service restaurant with a large selection of vegetarian dishes, but the waiting line is long (moderate).

Vegetariano: 41 Canuda, Tel. 302-1052. Closed Sundays and holidays. Good, small restaurant, but very crowded at lunchtime (moderate).

FAST FOOD
Drugtstore David: 19 Tuset. Here you can get a variety of hamburgers, pizzas, and Spanish meat meals. Especially popular among the young set.

McDonald's: 60-62 La Rambla, Tel. 317-9887.

Tropezien: 83 Passeig de Gràcia. This is a combination of a pizzeria and cafeteria.

HOME COOKING
El Corte Inglés: 14 Pl. de Catalunya. Lovely place, on the top floor of the famous department store (expensive).

Julivert Meu: 7 Bonsuccés, Tel. 318-0343. It looks small from the outside, but it is three storeys high. The bottom floor serves as a popular meeting place for young people, and the two upper floors are a typical local restaurant (inexpensive).

Pedro-Mary: 17 Carper de Ribes. Simple and pleasant workers' restaurant. Located next to the Arc del Triomf. Tasty food. Here, you will meet a cross-section of the local population (inexpensive).

Casa José: 10 Pl. Sant Josep Oriol. Closed Mondays. Its paella is very good. Meeting

An antique shop in the Gothic Quarter

place for backpackers and travellers with limited budgets (inexpensive).

Where to Shop and for What

The important shops in Barcelona are located in three main shopping areas:

In the old city – in Carrer del Pi, Portaferrissa, Av. Portal de l'Angel, Pelai, Carrer de la Palla streets, and all along las Ramblas.

In the Eixample Quarter – on Rambla de Catalunya and Passeig de Gràcia, considered Barcelona's "Fifth Avenue",

A rich variety of chocolates and sweets for those with a sweet tooth

where you will find Barcelona's most exclusive shops; also at the Pl. de Catalunya and the Rondas.

In the upper part of the city – Pl. Francesc Macia, Diagonal (here, too, is a concentration of the city's most elegant shops), Travessera de Gràcia, Vía Augusta, Fontestá, and Bori i.

It should be noted that most of Barcelona's shops hold sales during January and February and during July and August.

Prices in the most exclusive shops are high, as is the case in all the major cities of Europe. Note that in the large stores tourists are entitled to an exemption from VAT.

DEPARTMENT STORES
In the huge *El Corte Inglés* department store in the center of the city (14 Pl. de Catalunya) you can find a representative selection of the city's products at prices slightly lower than what is customary in the elegant boutiques. Open Mon.-Sat. from 10am-8pm continuously, without the noon break which is common in the other shops in the city, Tel. 302-1212.

This department store has a larger new branch at 617 Av. Diagonal. The variety of merchandise available in this department store is large and of good quality, Tel. 419-5206.

Galerías Preciados: 19 Av. Portal de l'Angel. Open Mon.-Fri. from 10am-8pm continuously and on Saturdays from 10am-9pm, Tel. 317-0000.

All department stores are closed on Sundays.

SHOPPING CENTERS

Barcelona is full of large shopping centers which have the advantage of offering many stores all under one roof. We suggest that you visit some of the largest of these centers.

Boulevard Rosa: 55 Passeig de Gràcia has over 100 different kinds of shops. Open every day from 10:30am-8:30pm except Sundays, Tel. 309-0650.

Cu-Cu: 13 Cucurulla, Tel. 301-4307. Mon.-Fri. 10:30am-2pm and 4:30-8:30pm, Sat. 10:30am-8:30pm.

La Avenida: 121 Rambla Catalunya. This center has almost 50 shops. Open Mon.-Sat. from 10:30am-2pm and from 4:30-8:30pm, Tel. 317-1398.

Diagonal Center: This is a very well-known center in Barcelona and includes 60 shops under one roof. It is located at 474 Av. Diagonal and is open every day except Sundays from 10:30am-2pm and 4:30-8:30pm, Tel. 309-0650.

Galeries Malda: A large center which has 60 shops, located at Pl. del Pi. The center is open for business every day (except Sundays) from 10am-1pm and 4-8:30pm.

ART OBJECTS AND ANTIQUES

In Barcelona you can buy good quality art objects and antiques, especially works from silver.

The Catalonian Association of Art Galleries: 77 Passeig de Gràcia, open during the usual business hours, Tel. 216-0003.

The Association of Antique Dealers of Catalonia: 223 Rosselló, Tel. 237-9656.

The Antique Center: Passeig de Gràcia (next to the *British Airways* office). This is a large exhibition and sales center for antiques with 75 shops, one next to another. The center is open Tues.-Sat. from 10:30am-2pm and on Mon.-Sat. from 4-8pm, Tel. 215-7178.

BOOKSTORES
The best bookstore for English and French books is *Llibreria Francesa*. This shop has a large selection of books on various subjects and is located at 91 Passeig de Gràcia, Tel. 215-1417. On the same street, at no. 79, is another recommended bookshop – *Happy Books*.

DRUGSTORES
for the "night owls" we recommend a visit to 71 Passeig de Gràcia, Tel. 487-2926 and 215-7074. At this address, there is a drugstore, open 24 hours a day. This drugstore includes 12 different kinds of shops: a restaurant, cafeteria, bar, supermarket, bookstore, gift shop, photography equipment store, billiards, etc.

Drugstore David: 19-21 Tuset , Tel. 209-6957. Open daily 9am-5am.

Vip's: 7 Rambla Catalunya, Tel. 317-4903. Open Sun-Thurs., 9am-1:30am; Fri.-Sat. 9am-3am.

MARKETS
People who enjoy open markets should not miss the **Els Encants**. The articles offered on sale here may not be "bargains", but the general atmosphere is happy and vibrant. The market is open Mon., Wed., Fri., and Sat. from 8am-7pm in winter and from

Shopping in the Gothic Quarter

8am-8pm in summer. It is located in Pl. de les Glóries and can be reached by the L1 subway (Glóries station).

There are other interesting markets in Barcelona, such as: the **antique market of the Gothic Quarter** located at Pl. del Pi. It is open every Thursday from 9am-8pm, except during the month of August.

The coin and stamp market is located at Pl. Reial and is open Sundays from 10am-2pm all year round.

The St. Anthony Market (Mercat de Sant Antoni) is located at the corner of Sant Pau and Sant Antoni streets. It has stalls with seafoods, and lots of vegetables, as well as textile products.

In addition, at this spot, on Sundays from 10am-2pm there is an **old coins and books market**. It can be reached vía the L3 subway (Poble Sec station).

In the **Spanish village** (Poble Espanyol) you can find many souvenirs typical of other regions of Spain, but they are not cheap and you may find them too "touristy" for your taste.

If you want to enjoy a colorful market with typical spanish foods, go to the Boqueria market, located between Carme and Hospital streets. It is open every day except Sundays.

SOUVENIRS
It is not easy to find souvenirs unique to Barcelona, but on the Ramblas you can find Indian shopkeepers who will be glad to sell you simple ordinary tourist items, such as printed

shirts, decorative dolls, boats in bottles, etc.

Night life

Up-to-date information about performances and concerts in Barcelona can be found in the weekly guide Guída del Ocio, sold at kiosks throughout the city and at tourist bureaus. Other sources of information are the entertainment columns

In Eixample Quarter one can find beautiful architecture and a variety of entertainment

in the daily papers *La Van-guardia* and *Diaro de Barcelona*. You may also phone directly to the various places listed below. In addition, there is a local

information service at Tel. 010, which is very efficient.
Remember that the demand for tickets to cultural events is greater than the supply, so you need to buy tickets in advance.

CLASSICAL MUSIC, DANCE

Classical music – most of the classical concerts in the city take place in the unique Palau de la Música Catalana auditorium at 1 Carrer Amadeu Vives, not far from the Plaça de Catalunya in the center of the city. There are many concerts held in this impressive auditorium, throughout the year, and most of the performances are first-rate. The ticket office is open all year except June and July from 11am-1pm and 5-7:45pm; in these two summer months, the ticket office is open only in the afternoons (Tel. 301-1104).

Dance – dance programs, especially modern dance performances, usually take place in the Mercat de les Flors theater at 59 Lleida Street or at the Institut del Teatre at 7 Sant Pere Més Baix. For more details phone 268-2078.

THEATER AND CINEMA
There are a number of theater companies in the city which present a variety of programs. All plays are in Spanish, so that this experience is limited to those who know Spanish. In the center of the city there are

a large number of movie theaters, modern and comfortable, which show movies from the United States and Western Europe. Before buying tickets, you should clarify whether the movie has been dubbed, a not uncommon practice.

The Barcelona cinematheque, *Filmoteca*, located at 63 Travessera de Gràcia (Tel. 201-2906), shows movies daily in their original languages, and also has a cinema library and archive.

NIGHTCLUBS AND DISCOTHEQUES

In Barcelona there are a large number of nightclubs offering cabaret performances, but only a few are top quality. The best (and the most expensive) of them is undoubtedly *Scala* at 47 Passeig de Sant Joan (Tel. 232-6363). The club has two performances nightly, one after 8pm and the other after midnight.

El Molino is an established nightclub, retaining the atmosphere of times past. It is located at 99 Vil i Vil (Tel. 241-6383), closed on Mondays.

Belle Epoque at 246 Muntaner (Tel. 209-7385) offers enjoyable performances and pleasant decor. Closed on Sundays.

The *Arnau* club is inexpensive and quite popular: in the heart of Barcelona's night life

district, at 60 Av. del Paral-lel (Tel. 242-2804). Closed on Wednesdays.

Discotheques are also popular in Barcelona, and there are many to be found all over the

city. One of the largest is *Studio 54*, next to *Club Arnau*, at 64 Av. del Paral-lel (open on Friday, Saturday, and Sunday).

Around the Diagonal, there are several discotheques: the most popular is *Bikini* at 571 Av. Diagonal (Tel. 230-5134).

Scores of night-clubs, discos etc. are listed in the Yellow Pages and in all dailies (in Spanish, look for *Salas de Fiestas Salazones* and *Discotecas*).

A dramatic dance – the flamenco

FLAMENCO

This famous Spanish dance is not so popular in Barcelona, the capital of Catalonia, since it is Andalusian. Still, you can have a taste of this kind of art, a soulful combination of music and dance.

The *Andalucia* club (Tel. 302-2029) and the *Cordobés* (Tel. 317-6653), next to each other, located at numbers 27 and 35 Rambla and the *Los Tarantos* club at 17 Pl. Reial (Tel. 318-3067) try to preserve the heritage of this famous Spanish dance. The performance at the *Tablao de Carmen Club* in Poble Espanyol is strictly for tourists.

CASINO

Gambling enthusiasts will have to travel away from Barcelona to the *Gran Casino Barcelona*, about 40 kms southwest of the city at Sant Pere de Ribes, near the town of Sitges (Tel. 893-3666). The casino is located in a pleasant building from the nineteenth century. For more details, phone 204-8014.

Those vacationing on Costa Brava or those ready to travel further afield from Barcelona will find two more casinos – the nearest one is located at Lloret del Mar and bears its name (Tel. 972-366512).

Sports

Football – The Barcelona football club has won many championships and awards and is greatly admired by the local population, which lovingly refers to the team as Barca. Their games are played in the Nou Camp Stadium which has

120,000 seats (see "Pedralbes" route). Tickets for the home games (once every two weeks between October and May) can be ordered at Tel. 330-9411. Adjoining the stadium is a special museum, documenting the history of the team and its achievements. A visit to the team museum also includes a visit to the football stadium.

The city's second football team, *Deportivo*, plays its home games at Sarriá Stadium, which has "only" 42,000 seats. It also has many fans in the city. Tickets can be ordered at Tel. 203-4800.

Basketball – The local basketball team is considered one of the best in Europe, and many fans come to see its games. Tickets to its home games, which take place in the local sports arena, can be ordered at Tel. 323-2216.

Auto racing – A number of auto races either take place or start out from Barcelona. The most well-known are the Monte-Carlo race in January and the Costa Brava race in February. Details about other races which take place in the area can be gotten by telephoning 200-3311.

Golf – The golf course closest to the city is Prat, about 15 kms from Barcelona, near the airport. At the golf course are also a restaurant, swimming pool, tennis courts, etc. For

Skiing at the artificial ski slope at the Piscina Municipal

more details and to make reservations, phone 379-0278.

Another golf course, a little further away, is at Sant Cugat del Valles, 20 kms from the city (Tel. 674-3958). Here, too, there is a swimmimg pool, a bar and a restaurant.

Tennis – The Barcelona tennis tournament, Conde de Godó, takes place in September every year at the Royal Tennis Club of Barcelona, 5 Bosch-l-Gimpera (Tel. 203-7852).

Tennis courts open to the public (for a fee) can be found at the Can Carlleu sports complex (Tel. 203-7874) and at the Vall Parc club (Tel. 212-6789).

Swimming – The Piscinas Bernat Picornell swimming pools were built for the 1970 XII European Swimming Championships. The sport complex has two Olympic pools, one indoor and the other outdoor, as well as a diving pool and various sport facilities.(30 Av. l'Estadi, Tel. 423-4041). The Piscina Municipal in Montjuïc, built in 1929, has been completely refurbished and has diving and waterpolo pools. It has a gymnasium as well as other facilities and is open to the public (31 Av. Miramar, Tel. 443-0046).

Squash – There are two good squash clubs in the city: *Squash Barcelona*, at 17 Av. Doctor Maranyon (Tel. 334-0258) and *Tibidabo Squash Club*, at 8 Llu's Muntadas (Tel. 212-4683). It is important to reserve your court in advance.

Skiing – During the winter season, a number of ski runs are open on the Pyrenees slopes, but most are several hundred kms from Barcelona. The nearest ski run is Port del Comte, about 120 kms away (Tel. 973-480481. Call to ask about weather conditions). In the Piscina Municipal (Municipal Swimming pool) in Montjuïc there is an artificial ski slope, made of PVC (Tel. 443-0046).

The Olympic Marina, designed and built as a major sports installation as well as an urban and public area, offers all possible services and attractions. You can get more information about other sports from the tourist information offices (see "Tourist services").

Important Addresses and Telephone Numbers

EMERGENCIES
National police: Tel. 091
Local police: Tel. 092
Central police station: 43
Rambla: Tel. 317-7020
Fire department: Tel. 080
Doctors: Tel. 212-8585
Ambulance services:
  Ajuntament (*SAMU*),
  Tel. 061
  Red Cross, Tel. 300-2020
  White Cross, Tel. 266-1212
  or 266-1266
  Catalunya, Tel. 422-8888
  or 422-8090
  Domingo, Tel. 278-0404,
  314-1212 or 314-4444
  Lazaro, Tel. 456-6666
  or 235- 4040
  Condal, Tel. 331-6666
  or 331-3636
  Seram, Tel. 337-8500
  Associació Barcelona Centre
  Mèdic, Tel. 414-0643
  Sant Pau Hospital: Tel.
  436-4711
Dental Treatment:
  Institut Dexeus, Tel.
  418-0000
  Amesa, Tel. 302-6682
  Clinicia Ever, Tel. 238-3161
  Clinicia Adesa, Tel. 458-4273

CONSULATES
Belgium: 303 Diputació,
Tel. 487-8140
Canada: 125 Vía Augusta,
Tel. 410-6699
France: 11 P. de Gràcia,
Tel. 317-8150

Germany: 111 P. de Gràcia,
Tel. 317-8150

Ireland: 94 Gran Vía Carles
III, Tel. 330-9652
Italy: 270 Mallorca, Tel.
488-0270
Holland: 601 Av. Diagonal,
Tel. 410-6210
Switzerland: 94 Gran Vía
Carles III, Tel. 330-9211
England: 477 Av. Diagonal,
Tel. 419-9044
United States: 23 Pg. Reina
Elisenda, Tel. 280-2227

CREDIT CARDS
Mastercharge/Visa: Tel.
315-2512
American Express: Tel.
572-0303
Diners' Club: Tel. 547-4000

COMMUNICATION AND TRANSPORTATION
Central post office: Plaça
Antoni López, at the end of
Vía Laietana, Tel. 318-3831
Telegraph office: Tel. 322-
2000 Road information: Tel.
204-2247
Telephone information: Tel.
003 Weather: Tel. 094
Public transportation:
Tel. 336-0000

Trains (*Renfe*): Tel. 322-4142
Lost and found: Tel. 318-9531,
317-3879
Taxis: Tel. 330-0804
Airport: Tel. 379-2454,
379-2762
Auto repairs and towing
service (24 hours a day):
Tel. 350-7535, 351-1203
Transmediterránea: Tel.
412-2524

AIRLINES
Iberia: 30 Passeig de Gràcia,
Tel. 301-3993
Air France: 63 Passeig de
Gràcia, Tel. 487-2526
British Airways: 85 Passeig de
Gràcia, Tel. 487-2112.
KLM: 262 Calle Muntaner,
Tel. 379-5458
Lufthansa: 55 Passeig de
Gràcia, Tel. 487-0300
Sabena: 78 Passeig de Gràcia,
Tel. 487-4779
Swissair: 44 Passeig de Gràcia,
Tel. 215-9100

TWA: 55 Passeig de Gràcia,
Tel. 215-2188
Delta: 16 Passeig de Gràcia,
Tel. 412-4333
Alitalia: 403 Diagonal,
Tel. 416-0424.

BARCELONA OFFICES OF TOURISM ABROAD:
Amsterdam, Tel. 685-0401
Athens, Tel. 323-7524
Berlin, Tel. (01) 306-363
Boston, Tel. (800) 772-4642
Brussels, Tel. (02) 512-0817
Copenhagen, Tel. (33) 122-222
Stockohlm, Tel. 823-7875
Frankfurt, Tel. (069) 728-254
Helsinki, Tel. 640-966
London, Tel. (071) 437-5622
Miami, Tel. 305-8880
Montreal, Tel. (514) 849-3352
Munich, Tel. (01) 306-363
New York, Tel. (800) 772-4642
Tokyo, Tel. (03) 582-3831
Washington, Tel.
(800) 772-4642
Zurich, Tel. 221-1425

Dictionary

In order to facilitate the use of this dictionary we added the proper pronounciation of some of the catalan words in brackets.

English	Spanish	Catalan
good morning	*buenos días*	*bon dia*
hello/good bye	*hola, adiós*	*hola, adéusiau*
good evening	*buenas tardes*	*bona tarda*
good night	*buenas noches*	*bona nit*
please	*por favor*	*si us plau (-oos-plaoo)*
thank you	*gracias*	*gràcies*
pardon, excuse	*perdón*	*perdó*
yes	*sí*	*sí*
non	*no*	*no*
what...?	*qué...?*	*què...?*
when...?	*cuándo?*	*quan?*
where...?	*dónde?*	*on?*
there is...	*hay*	*hi ha (e a)*
there is not...	*no hay*	*no hi ha*
what is the time?	*Qué hora es?*	*Quina hora és? (kina ora)*
how are you?	*Cómo estás?*	*Com estàs?*
far	*lejos*	*lluny (iooñ)*
near	*cerca*	*a prop*
big/large	*grande*	*gran*
small	*pequeño*	*petit*
new	*nuevo*	*nou (naoo)*
old	*antiguo/viejo*	*antic/vell*
right	*izquierda*	*esquerra (asquerra)*
left	*derecha*	*dreta*
first	*primero*	*primer (prime-)*
last	*último*	*darrer (darre-)*
open	*abierto*	*obert (oobert)*
closed	*cerrado*	*tancat*
entrance	*entrada*	*entrada (antrada)*
exit	*salida*	*sortida (soortida)*

English	Spanish	Catalan
bus	*autobus*	*autobus (autoboos)*
bus station	*parada del autobus*	*parada de l'autobus*
train	*tren*	*tren*
subway/ underground	*metro*	*metro (metroo)*
railway station	*parada del tren*	*parada del tren*
ticket	*billete*	*bitllet (bit-let)*
taxi	*taxi*	*taxi*
car	*coche*	*cotxe (cotcha)*
plane	*avión*	*avió*
airport	*aeropuerto*	*aeroport*
boat/ship	*barco*	*vaixell (va-shel)*
port/quay/wharf	*puerto/muelle*	*pont/moll*
slow	*despacio*	*a poc a poc*
fast	*deprisa*	*depressa*
gas	*gasolina*	*benzina*
gas station	*surtidor de gasolina*	*sortidor de benzina*
hotel	*hotel*	*hotel (ootel)*
hostel	*albergue*	*hospederia (oospadaria)*
room	*habitación*	*habitació/cambra*
toilets	*servicios*	*lavabos (lavaboos)*
bath/shower	*baño/ducha*	*bany/dutxa (bañ/doocha)*
restaurant	*restaurante*	*restaurant (restaoorant)*
café	*café/bar*	*cafè/bar*
table	*mesa*	*taula (taoola`*
chair	*silla*	*cadira*
waiter	*camarero*	*cambrer (kambre-)*
water	*agua*	*aigua (i-gooa)*
bread	*pan*	*pa*
drink	*bebida*	*beguda (bagooda)*
menu	*menú*	*menu (ma-noo)*
hot	*caliente*	*calent*
cold	*frio*	*fred*
soup	*sopa*	*sopa*
meat	*carne*	*carn*
salad	*ensalada*	*amanida*
bill	*cuenta*	*compte*
receipt	*recibo*	*rebut (raboot)*

English	Spanish	Catalan
cinema	*cine*	*cinema*
theatre	*teatro*	*teatre (teatra)*
pharmacy	*farmacia*	*farmàcia*
shop, store	*tienda*	*botiga (bootiga)*
newsstand	*kiòsko*	*kiòsk*
post office	*correos*	*correu*
hospital	*hospital*	*hospital (oospital)*
police	*policia*	*policia (poolicia)*
embassy	*embajada*	*ambaixada (amba-shada)*
market, bazaar	*mercado*	*mercat*
how much does it cost?	*cuánto cuesta?*	*qué val?*
expensive	*caro*	*car*
cheap	*barato*	*barat*
road, highway	*carretera, autopista*	*carretera, autopista*
street	*calle*	*carrer (care-)*
avenue	*avenida*	*avinguda (avingooda)*
square	*plaza*	*plaça*
alley	*callejuela*	*carrero (carraro)*
esplanade	*paseo*	*passeig (passaig)*
bridge	*puente*	*pont*
monument	*monumento*	*monument*
fountain	*fuente*	*font*
church	*iglesia*	*església (esglezia)*
palace	*palacio*	*palau*
fort/castle	*castillo*	*castell*
town/city	*ciudad*	*ciutat*
village	*pueblo*	*poble (popla)*
museum	*museo*	*museu*
park	*jardin público*	*jardí públic*
east	*este*	*est*
north	*norte*	*nord*
west	*oeste*	*uest*
south	*sur*	*sud*
valley	*valle*	*vall*
mountain	*montaña*	*muntanya (moontania)*
range	*cordillera*	*carena*
hill	*colina*	*turó*

English	Spanish	Catalan
forest	*bosque*	*bosc*
river	*rio*	*riu*
Sunday	*Domingo*	*Diumenge (dioomenja)*
Monday	*Lunes*	*Dilluns (di-ioons)*
Tuesday	*Martes*	*Dimarts (dimars)*
Wednesday	*Miércoles*	*Dimecres (dimekras)*
Thursday	*Jueves*	*Dijous (dijaoos)*
Friday	*Viernes*	*Divendres (divendras)*
Saturday	*Sábado*	*Dissabte (disapta)*
January	*Enero*	*Gener (jane-)*
February	*Febrero*	*Febrer (fabre-)*
March	*Marzo*	*Març (mars)*
April	*Abril*	*Avril*
May	*Mayo*	*Maig (match)*
June	*Junio*	*Juny (jooni)*
July	*Julio*	*Juliol (jooliol)*
August	*Agosto*	*Agost*
September	*Septiembre*	*Setembre (setembra)*
October	*Octubre*	*Octubre (ooctoobra)*
November	*Noviembre*	*Novembre (noovembra)*
December	*Diciembre*	*Decembre (dazembra)*
one	*uno/una*	*un/una (oon/oona)*
two	*dos*	*dos/dues (dos/dooas)*
three	*tres*	*tres*
four	*cuatro*	*quatre (quatra)*
five	*cinco*	*cinc*
six	*seis*	*sis*
seven	*siete*	*set*
eight	*ocho*	*vuit (vooit)*
nine	*nueve*	*nou (nao)*
ten	*diez*	*deu (deoo)*
eleven	*once*	*onze (onza)*

English	Spanish	Catalan
twelve	*doce*	*dotze (doza)*
thirteen	*trece*	*tretze (tre-za)*
fourteen	*catorce*	*catorze (catorza)*
fifteen	*quince*	*quinze (quinza)*
sixteen	*dieciseis*	*setze (setza)*
seventeen	*diecisiete*	*disset*
eighteen	*dieciocho*	*divuit*
nineteen	*diecinueve*	*dinou (dinaoo)*
twenty	*veinte*	*vint*
twenty-one	*veintiuno*	*vint-i-ú*
thirty	*trenta*	*trenta*
thirty-one	*trentiuno*	*trentiu*
forty	*cuarenta*	*quaranta (qooranta)*
fifty	*cincuenta*	*cinquanta*
sixty	*sesenta*	*seixanta (sheshanta)*
seventy	*setenta*	*setanta*
eighty	*ochenta*	*vuitanta*
ninety	*noventa*	*noranta (nooranta)*
hundred	*cien*	*cent*
hundred and one	*ciento uno*	*cent ú (cent-òo)*
hundred and ten	*ciento diez*	*cent deu (-deoo)*
two hundreds	*doscientos/as*	*dos-cents/ dues-centes (centas)*
three hundreds	*trescientos*	*tres-cents*
four hundreds	*quatrocientos*	*quatre-cents*
five hundreds	*quinientos*	*cinc-cents*
six hundreds	*seiscientos*	*sis-cents*
seven hundreds	*setecientos*	*set-cents*
eight hundreds	*ochocientos*	*vuit-cents*
nine hundreds	*nuevecientos*	*nou-cents (naoo-)*
thousand	*mil*	*mil*
two thousand	*dos mil*	*dos mil*
million	*un millón*	*un milió*

INDEX

R

S

T

INDEX

NOTES

NOTES

QESTIONNAIRE

In our efforts to keep up with the pace and pulse of Barcelona, we kindly ask your cooperation in sharing with us any information which you may have as well as your comments. We would greatly appreciate your completing and returning the following questionnaire. Feel free to add additional pages.

Our many thanks!

To: Inbal Travel Information (1983) Ltd.
18 Hayetzira st.
Ramat Gan 52521
Israel

Name: _____

Address: _____

Occupation: _____

Date of visit: _____

Purpose of trip (vacation, business, etc.): _____

Comments/Information: _____

_____

_____

_____

_____

_____

_____

INBAL Travel Information Ltd.
P.O.B 1870 Ramat Gan
ISRAEL 52117